Values and Violence in Auschwitz

ANNA PAWEŁCZYŃSKA

Translated and with an Introduction
by Catherine S. Leach

University of California Press   Berkeley · Los Angeles · London

Values and Violence in Auschwitz

A SOCIOLOGICAL ANALYSIS

Translated from the Polish edition: *Wartości A Przemoc. Zarys socjologicznej problematyki Oświęcimia* by Anna Pawełczyńska (Warsaw: Państwowe Wydawnictwo Naukowe, 1973)

University of California Press
Berkeley and Los Angeles, California
University of California Press, Ltd.
London, England
Copyright © 1979 by
The Regents of the University of California
First Paperback Printing 1980
ISBN 0-520-04242-5
Library of Congress Catalog Card Number: 76-3886
Printed in the United States of America

1   2   3   4   5   6   7   8   9

TO MOTHERS

Contents

List of Illustrations   ix

Translator's Introduction   xi

Author's Introduction   1

1. The World Outside the Camp: Frames of Reference   6
The Authority of Terror   7
Defense of the Dimension of Life   10

2. Institutions of State Crime   15

3. Living Space   24
At Home   25
The Road to Work   35
Space and Communication   42

4. Breaking the Prisoners' Solidarity   44

5. Social Differentiation and the Odds for Survival   51
Unequal Chances on Arrival   52
Unequal Chances of Defense   59

6. A Place in the Structure of Terror   68
Penal Crews   69
The Privileges of Relative Stability   69
Ambiguous Privileges   72
Muselmänner—Beyond Chance and Judgment   74

Industrial Death   77
The Elite   80

7. The Psychological Relativity of Numbers   83
Size of the Apparatus of Violence   84
Colored Triangles   85
Letters and Numbers   89

8. Love and Erotica   94

9. Socio-Economic Defense Mechanisms   100
The Function and Evolution of the
    Camp Market   101
The Battle for Power   106

10. The Organized Resistance Movement   112

11. Mechanisms of Adaptation and Self-Defense   123
The Social Experiment   123
Reduction of Material Needs   127

12. People and Values   135
Values as a Frame of Reference   136
The Reinterpretation of Moral Standards   137

Glossary   145   Bibliographical Note   149   Index   151

Illustrations

1. Plan of Auschwitz I.   26
2. Plan of Auschwitz II—Birkenau.   27
3. Dimensions of bunk beds.   29
4. Dimensions of roosts.   29
5. Sketch plan of crematory III in Auschwitz II—Birkenau.   31

Map 1. The German Partition of Poland.   x
Map 2. Distances to work sites outside camp.   32

Plate 1. Auschwitz barracks in winter.   36
Plate 2. Close up of Auschwitz barracks.   36
Plate 3. Bunk beds.   37
Plate 4. Bunk beds.   38
Plate 5. Roosts.   39
Plate 6. Main entrance to Auschwitz I, with inscription, *Arbeit macht frei.*   39

Map 1. The German Partition of Poland, 1931/41–1945. (Adapted from Lucy S. Dawidowicz, *The War Against the Jews* [Bantam, 1976], p. 151.)

Translator's Introduction

A NNA PAWEŁCZYŃSKA was born in 1922 in Poland
into a middle-class family. Had it not been for the
outbreak of World War II in September 1939, she
would have entered her senior year of high school, completed the
normal course of studies and officially graduated. Instead she
helped set up an army field hospital, where she worked during
the September campaign. After the Germans occupied Poland
she organized an aid program for wounded Polish soldiers.

Her birthdate and her reaction to the German invasion indicate that she belonged to the historically conscious younger generation of Poles who took the invasion as a tragic continuation of
Poland's past. In her study the author attaches a special importance to the nature of the Polish historical process as it affected
both parents and children of the Hitler era. A brief exposition of
the substance of events leading from the text's furthest point of

reference in time, the period of Poland's political dismember-
ment known as the Partition Era, may therefore be of use to the
reader.

The Commonwealth of Poland and Lithuania was one of the
great European powers until the end of the seventeenth century.
The eighteenth century witnessed the total eclipse of this extraordinary state, and within the space of twenty-three years, from
1772 to 1795, three successive partitions were imposed by its
mightier neighbors, Austria, Prussia, and Russia. The subject of
countless studies by Polish historians, the partitions have been
evaluated in terms of both accusatory and recriminatory theories, the first placing full blame on the domestic doorstep, the
second faulting indifferent allies and treacherous enemies.
Present-day scholarship seeks not to indict but to understand
the mechanisms and interrelations of the internal processes
which led to the extinction of the Polish state at the hands of
Austria, Prussia, and Russia. Today the problem tends to be
viewed as the result of the conflict between Poland's growing
desire for social reform (as evidenced in political and social reform movements, the currency of enlightened ideas, and an
energetic political leadership) and the desire of her powerful
neighbors to maintain a status quo (i.e., serfdom, political iner-
tia, abuses of gentry democracy, opposition to constitutional
reform) which lent itself to foreign manipulation.

At the time of the partitions, Poland found herself in a very
weak position caused by internal difficulties and the lack of a
true professional standing army. The younger generation, in-
spired by the ideas of the Enlightenment, the French Revolution,
and the American Revolution, was full of plans for the reform of
Polish political, economic, and social institutions. Thus when
the partitioning powers abruptly stifled this energy—imprisoning
the most influential leaders, excluding the citizenry from the
exercise of political control, prolonging the servitude of the
peasant, instituting policies of cultural discrimination and, at
different periods, police terror—much of the nation reacted with
anger and resentment.

In defiance many Poles turned to clandestine activity in secret organizations and to alliances with revolutionary movements throughout Europe, such as the Decembrists in Russia, the 1848 revolutions, and the Paris Commune; others sought openly to enlist the aid of established Western powers. Napoleon, for example, was offered a fighting force in the shape of Polish legions. None of these strategies bore fruit, and two domestic armed rebellions, one in 1830, the other in 1863, ended in disaster.

Although defeat brought a change of focus to Polish attitudes—from flamboyant defiance to sober positivism—the Poles never reconciled themselves to partition. The price was too dear: the suppression of the Polish language and culture, deportation and exile for the insurgents, the abolition of the army and native political institutions, and the use of police terror. To a large extent, it was the Polish Catholic church, the only organized force permitted to exist in the partitioned country, which kept the sense of national identity and common destiny alive. But news from abroad of the accomplishments of Polish artists, writers, and musicians in exile and the activity of intellectuals and activists at home also maintained national awareness and pride. Though marked by failed uprisings and severe reprisals, a century and a half of partition never succeeded in atomizing the Poles. Rather it forged a common will to survive as a nation, which first took hold with the middle gentry, then passed to the intellectuals and business sector, and by the twentieth century had spread throughout all of Polish society.

When, at last, after World War I, an independent Polish state was reborn, the necessary determination was available to protect the cherished dream of independence. When both western partitioning powers (Austria and Germany) collapsed as a result of internal revolts, the Poles moved quickly to clear the country of German and Austrian soldiers. In the east, although the Bolsheviks had abrogated all partition treaties after Imperial Russia ceased to exist following the October Revolution of 1917, the Poles challenged Soviet Russia's seizure of Lithuanian and Ukrainian territories which were felt to belong to Poland by virtue of their having been part of the former Commonwealth of Poland and Lithuania (rendered extinct by the partitions). A Polish army with the charismatic Józef Piłsudski in command fought to recover these lands. Many Polish soldiers carried the fight against the Bolsheviks inside Russia itself, but more significant was Poland's reaction (in the face of allied indecision) to the 1920 Soviet advance which threatened the Polish capital itself. The internal squabbles plaguing the new government were put aside as the whole nation rallied to Marshal Piłsudski's summons for volunteers. Many thousands joined up for crash military training, while noncombatants carried the call to town and countryside through meetings, posters, and pamphlets. Poland's counteroffensive came off brilliantly, aided at the last moment by Allied supplies and French military personnel, and although the boundary question was not settled in accordance with Polish aspirations (ethnic Lithuania became an independent state and survived until 1939, while most of the Ukraine remained under Soviet rule), Poland had fought for and preserved her new political independence.

It was this tradition which stood behind what Pawełczyńska calls the "great national mobilization" which began as soon as the German army invaded Poland. After the defeat the majority of Polish officers and soldiers went underground to organize armed resistance among the citizenry. The Polish underground was the first in Europe to take up arms against the Nazis. Masses of boys and girls, their high schools and colleges closed down by the occupier, rushed to join the underground army—known as the Home Army—and other clandestine groups. Pawełczyńska herself soon became a member of the Resistance and acted as a carrier for the underground press and also as a liaison for one of the officers of the Home Army in the Warsaw district. In addition she attended clandestine study sessions to prepare for her final examinations. Such illegal educational activity was carried on at great risk by school and university authorities throughout the occupation. While the author was taking her exams, the Gestapo arrested the group of instructors.

From the beginning of the occupation, Poland, like other occupied countries, was treated to the ruthless application of Nazi "justice." Once more Poland was dismembered—the consequence of a secret clause in the Molotov-Ribbentrop Pact between Germany and Russia. Germany incorporated Poland's western provinces (including the Auschwitz area) and Danzig directly into the Third Reich. This territory was destined for immediate resettlement with Germans. As the German army advanced, certain "hostile elements" among the civilians from these provinces (political leaders, teachers, priests, landowners, etc.) were summarily executed by special squads; civilian refugees were bombed and strafed; mass expulsions of approximately 5 million Jews and Poles considered unsuitable for Germanization were carried out (about 25,000 members of the intelligentsia were shot during the resettlement); Polish and Jewish property was confiscated, and nearly two and a half million Poles were deported to the German Reich for forced labor. Against the Poles who were allowed to remain, intense discrimination was given force of law: deprivation of political, property, and trading rights; closure of secondary schools and colleges; a ban on all cultural and sports activity, and on religious services in Polish. A sort of colony or reservation for Poles was created out of central Poland. It was known as the Government General and included the towns of Kraków, Warsaw, Lublin, Radom and, later, Lwów. The Soviet Union took over the eastern provinces, with Vilno and Lwów, until the invading Germans overran them in the summer of 1941. These actions initiated some six years of unprecedented, systematic terror.

As in the development of resistance movements in other Nazi-occupied countries of Europe, the initial impulses of Polish resistance stemmed from an instinctive patriotism, but Nazi behavior could not be observed for long without provoking moral conviction. Thus Chamberlain's sentiment, expressed when Britain declared war on Germany on 3 September 1939, was shared by all the nations who subsequently fought in the "shadow wars" of the Resistance: "It is evil things we shall be fighting against, brute force, bad faith, injustice, oppression, and persecution. But against them I am certain the right will prevail."

Terror was applied in all occupied countries. Usually only those citizens who actively resisted the occupiers, or who were under suspicion of being activists, incurred death, torture, or deportation to a concentration camp. But in Poland everyone was subject to such brutality, and mass executions based on the principle of collective guilt were far more frequent, because every Pole, regardless of age, sex, or health, was a member of a condemned nation—condemned by the policy-makers in the Nazi party and government. Thus, in a speech to the *Wehrmacht* high command on 22 August 1939, Hitler declared, "the object of war is . . . physically to destroy the enemy. That is why I have prepared, for the moment only in the East, my 'Death's Head' formations with orders to kill without pity or mercy all men, women, and children of Polish descent or language. Only in this way can we obtain the living space we need."[1]

The *Generalplan Ost* (whose existence came to light in captured Nazi documents and whose final version had been formulated in 1940) contained both short and long-range plans for the "East" (that is, Poland, Czechoslovakia, the Baltic countries, Russia, Byelorussia, the Ukraine and the Crimea). Ultimately, it called for the gradual evacuation and dispersement of 80 to 85 percent of the Poles from their historical lands into Siberia, the elimination of the intelligentsia through emigration, and the acceptance of a small percentage of Poles "suitable for Germanization" who would be allowed to remain. The Poles were characterized as having a high sense of patriotism, a hostile attitude to Germany, and a natural bent for underground activity which rendered them intractable. During the war, however, Hitler's

1. Adolf Hitler, speech to top Wehrmacht officers, Obersalzberg, 22 August 1939, Document L-003 of the Nürnberg International Military Tribunal, cited in Janusz Gumkowski and Kazimierz Leszczyński, *Poland under Nazi Occupation* (Warsaw: Polonia, 1961), p. 59.

policy was to use the Poles in the Government General as a reservoir of manpower, and to exterminate the intelligentsia entirely. The treatment of Poles throughout the occupation leaves little doubt that the aim of Nazi policy was to destroy Polish national identity and to force Poles into the role of serfs to German masters. Himmler was explicit: "For the non-German population of the East, there can be no type of school above the four-grade elementary school. The job of these schools should be confined to the teaching of counting (no higher than to 500), the writing of one's name, and the teaching that God's commandment means obedience to the Germans, honesty, diligence and politeness. Reading I do not consider essential."[2]

It is probably not an exaggeration to say that nowhere was Nazi systematic oppression and terror applied with more viciousness than in Poland. In the Government General, Poles were removed from higher administrative posts in government and business. With the influx of millions of Poles and Jews from the western provinces, the standard of living was deliberately allowed to sink to the near-starvation level. Health services were reduced to inadequacy. The economic base was plundered, as businesses, factories, estates, and corporate securities were confiscated and raw materials exploited. With the closing of the secondary schools and institutions of higher learning, the prohibition against the publication of Polish newspapers and books, and the ban on every kind of cultural organization, the intelligentsia was deprived of legal employment and thus became susceptible to arrest. On the other hand the lowest types of diversions were encouraged—gambling, burlesque theaters, pornography, prostitution, drunkenness. No other European country under Nazi occupation was deprived of the right to its art and culture. In Poland the Nazis carried out systematic destruction

2. Heinrich Himmler, "Some Comments on the Treatment of Foreign Nationals in the East," a "highly confidential" 6-page typescript, signed and dated 15 May 1940, *Records of the Trial of Joseph Bühler* before the Supreme National Tribunal, vol. VI, pp. 65ff, cited by Janusz Gumkowski and Kazimierz Leszczyński in *Poland under Nazi Occupation* (Warsaw: Polonia, 1961), p. 30.

and plundering of national monuments, libraries, churches, and museums—in short, the humiliation of everything Polish.

The more acute forms of terror included mass executions of civilians, prisoners, and army officers; torture by the Gestapo; street round-ups of random, innocent civilians for deportation to the Reich or to concentration camps to be exploited as slave labor; massive deportations of whole towns and villages from the eastern territories (e.g., Zamość) to concentration camps or the Reich (in all about 2,460,000 Poles were sent to Germany); and mass kidnapping of children for Germanization and forced labor in the Reich. Finally, the holocaust of Europe's Jews took place on Polish territory.

In view of this systematically destructive policy toward the Poles and the attitude which saw the Slav as a subhuman, a criminal, and an enemy of Germany, it is perhaps more than conjecture that had the Nazis been victorious the Poles would have suffered the same fate as the Jews. Poland was the first country to be subjected to Hitler's "negative demographic policy," whose purpose was to prepare the vast territories in "The East" for German resettlement, and Poland suffered the greatest losses in life of all the occupied countries—220 per 1000 inhabitants. Polish sources state that no less than 6,028,000 Polish citizens, of whom 3,200,000 were Jews, lost their lives. Of this total, only 10.7 percent were war casualties. The rest (89.9 percent) perished as a result of Nazi terror in camps, ghettos, pacifications, executions, prisons, from injuries, overwork, and malnutrition. Chief target of the campaign against the Polish nation was the intelligentsia (including the clergy), who perished in the hundreds of thousands in executions and various types of camps.

Pawełczyńska was arrested by the Gestapo in August 1942 and imprisoned in Pawiak prison; she endured the torture of interrogation and was sent without a sentence to the concentration camp at Auschwitz-Birkenau, classified as a Polish political prisoner. During her sojourn in that camp she was a member of an organized resistance movement. In October 1944 she was transported to Flossenbürg in Germany, where she worked in a factory. In April 1945, during the evacuation of the camp, she escaped from the transport and took cover in the woods; some forced labor deportees took care of her. Later, in May and June of that year, she helped run a program assisting Poles in Germany to return to their country. Finally at the end of June she herself left for Poland.

Like other concerned survivors of the camps, Anna Pawełczyńska must have been driven by an urgent desire to participate in the remaking of the "good society." Immediately upon her return she enrolled at the University of Warsaw to study sociology. In the Poland to which she returned, political power had passed to those who proclaimed the new order of the East and professed the ideology of Karl Marx (which, though conceived in and for the West, was being freely adapted by the Soviet Union). The appeal of Marxism, with its seemingly realistic hopes of liberating the oppressed, transforming social relations, even man himself, must have been keen for many people after the war, in whose view liberalism had failed. On the other hand the fact that the Soviet Union was the guardian of those hopes must have tinged them with a dark anxiety.

Those fears proved to be justified. In this connection it may be noted that Marxist sociology has not had favorable conditions in which to develop in Eastern European countries. The unique political dangers inherent in Marxism's claims to be both an objective social science and the doctrine of a particular social class became fully apparent in the Stalinist era. Empirical investigations into society were hardly encouraged, while theory was often bent to meet political exigencies. Free inquiry was eclipsed by dogmatic assertion. Since the "Thaw" (1956), sociology in the people's democracies has made a comeback, but neither as the vanguard of Marxist thought nor in opposition to it, for its concerns and methods of research are not much different from those elsewhere in the industrialized (or industrializing) world.

Pawełczyńska's work for both the master's (1950) and doctor's

(1960) degrees was directed by the distinguished Polish sociologist, Stanisław Ossowski (1897–1963), who is today regarded as having been one of the more creative social scientists in the communist world. She also taught at the University of Warsaw (1957–1960) while Ossowski occupied the chair of sociology there.

Ossowski was mainly a theorist. His work did not lead him to conclusions widely divergent from those of sociologists elsewhere, but it was important for Polish sociology, especially his profound reappraisal of Marx's class theory, *Class Structure in the Social Consciousness* (New York: Free Press, 1963), which distinguishes the various conceptions of class contained in Marx's theory, establishes the tentative nature of Marx's synthesis, and shows its evolutionary potential if only it is not accepted as dogma. Thus Ossowski arrived at the "un-Marxist" view that social stratification in all modern industrial societies is increasingly determined by the political authorities, instead of vice versa.

Because Pawełczyńska credits the thirty years that separate her and the subject of *Values and Violence* with providing a perspective in which objectivity at least became a possibility, it is worth presenting the personal and public events of the period, which were important for shaping that perspective.

Certainly Ossowski exercised a primary influence. Her sociological study of Auschwitz embraces philosophical, political, moral, legal, medical, and psychological aspects and considers their interrelatedness, thereby attesting to a respect for Marx's profound view of human societies as "wholes or systems in which social groups, institutions, beliefs, and doctrines are interrelated." Her study also reveals that, like Ossowski, she rejects a rigid Marxism that would end up in a doctrinaire apology for the status quo. Thus the role she assigns to values in the historical process might (but not necessarily) lead toward a liberal interpretation of history, or it might be the beginning of a synthesis of Marxist and liberal methods. Her proposal that politicians use the lesson of the camps (which teaches that no end justifies every means) as a check on their activity is also noteworthy in this context, as is her analysis in chapter twelve of the moral problems of Auschwitz, which discredits a simplistic interpretation of the Marxist axiom "existence determines consciousness."

From Ossowski, Pawełczyńska learned to combine a precise conceptual framework and expository style with rigorous inductive analysis, and to view the results from a broad historical and cultural perspective. This method has made it possible for her to come to grips with a problem few scholars have been able (or willing) to tackle. It has enabled her to present the problems of the concentration camp in social categories familiar to everyone, while the richness of documentation (see Polish edition), which includes specialized scholarly studies, guarantees that her experience of the facts can be compared and expanded to the point where generalization becomes possible. What sets her study apart are the precise distinctions on which she bases her judgments— her analyses, for example, of spatial factors and communications, of the role of small groups, of the behavior of the *Muselmänner*, of the function of the camp market. Through her complete avoidance of naturalism (which, by sparing the mind the paralyzing effects of horror, enables it to penetrate to inner laws) and her perspective as a cultural anthropologist, she succeeds in viewing the concentration camp in the context of the most basic values of European culture (or "Western civilization"). And thus she brings her subject out of its isolation and neglect into the realm of contemporary social awareness.

The author spent the Stalinist years conducting field studies on juvenile delinquency as part of a research team in the Criminology Section of the Polish Academy of Sciences' Institute of Legal Studies. The year of the "Thaw" she spent in France as a visiting sociologist at the Institute of Demography and Public Opinion Research. On her return to Poland she immediately set about organizing the first Public Opinion Research Center in the Socialist-bloc countries, which she directed until 1964. The center was responsible for accumulating valuable survey data about cultural and social change in Poland, about behavior patterns in different social roles and different kinds of situations, and about the mechanisms of attitude and value formation. Several university institutes cooperated with the center, with the result that many worthwhile books about postwar social change were written.

Toward the end of this period Pawełczyńska wrote her doctoral dissertation on *Crime Among Juvenile Groups* (published 1964) based on her intensive empirical studies. It combined comprehensive investigation of groups of juvenile delinquents with an attempt to discover general laws governing the origin, structure, and functioning of these groups.

Until 1969 she was concerned with problems of culture, working in the Research on Contemporary Culture Workshop at the Academy of Sciences' Institute of Literary Research and as a member of the Commission of Experts for the Ministry of Art and Culture and the Planning Commission. In 1966 her dissertation on *The Dynamics of Cultural Change in Rural Society* for the *"habilitacja"* (Poland's highest academic degree, conferring the title of Docent) was accepted by the Department of Philosophy at the University of Warsaw. Her work, both in method and subject matter, was innovative in Poland. Using official statistics on the processes of industrialization and urbanization, as well as the data on values, attitudes, and outlooks on life that she had collected during her many years as head of the Public Opinion Research Center, and statistical data on more objective cultural phenomena, Pawełczyńska produced profiles of Poland's territorial units and, by means of ecological correlations, analyzed the main trends of cultural change. Her primary conclusion was that only if changes of an urbanizing nature occur in the social infrastructure, can it be said that industrialization produces essential cultural changes in rural society. Two related works, *Studies of Readership* and *Urbanization of Polish Culture*, were subsequently published in 1969.

Since then Pawełczyńska has devoted herself to the problems of values and lifestyles, while working with the Social Prognostics

Group at the Academy of Sciences' Institute of Philosophy and Sociology. She has also directed a series of field study projects on the subject of leisure for the Commission on Physical Culture and Tourism and acted as a scientific consultant for studies on foreign travel conducted in cooperation with the German Democratic Republic. *Values and Violence* was published in 1973. It won the coveted Ossowski award of the Polish Sociological Association.

To appreciate the book's reception in Poland requires some knowledge of the historical context. The quantity of original writing in Polish on the concentration camps is mountainous. A few items have appeared in English translation. Most of the material, as in other languages, has a documentary character— eyewitness accounts, memoirs, letters, reports, scientific articles, sources and documents published by Poland's War Crimes Investigation Commission and various other institutes and organizations specializing in collecting data and publishing material relating to the camps. A handful of scholars have written books on selected aspects. The remainder consists of literary works in various genres—diary, memoir, poetry, drama, novel, short story. Most authors, as in other countries, saw themselves, above all, as bearers of witness to atrocious crimes and unimaginable sufferings. Their interpretations of their experience range from mystical-religious to angry naturalism. Attempts to seek meaning in a religious mystique of suffering were bitterly "exposed" and harshly castigated by those who were convinced of the senselessness of that suffering, and who saw it as the consequence of purely human evil and purely "human stupidity for getting caught," or as a result of what Camus called "humanists . . . not [being] careful enough." The effect upon the reader of this literature is often so brutal that the mind is numbed, overwhelmed.

The most durable artistic effort at depicting concentration camp reality in Polish, or perhaps in any language, is Tadeusz Borowski's cycle of short stories on Auschwitz, *This Way for the*

Gas, Ladies and Gentlemen (London: Penguin, 1976). No other writer has been able to expose with such precision the mechanisms of degradation. At the time of its publication (1946), Borowski's naked writing was mistaken by many Polish readers for moral nihilism. Few perceived that his fear of distorting the truth, his desire to prevent the birth of myths and legends (whether surrounding victims or aggressors), and rage against a world of evil had led him to neglect transcendence. The controversy over the interpretation of camp experience locked Catholic and Marxist critics into a conflict between idealism and realism. During this debate Borowski remarked, "In writing about large historical movements, in writing about great moral upheavals, in writing about Auschwitz, one cannot use other than purely human categories, couched in a verifiable vocabulary."

Until Pawełczyńska, no one else successfully followed the spirit of his advice and no one managed to overcome the conflict. Her study therefore marks a breakthrough—in her reevaluation of materialist and idealist concepts, and in her analysis of the interrelated mechanisms of terror and resistance. It also confirms the validity of Borowski's artistic judgment. Pawełczyńska's vocabulary and style, her use of categories like "home," "living space," "market," "communication," with which everyone is familiar, that are tailored to human size, make it possible for those "who never met with concentration camp reality" to *understand*.

When the reviews of *Values and Violence* appeared in Poland, the earlier ideological controversy could not help but be present between the lines. Catholic reviewers displayed high levels of enthusiasm, while the Marxist press nodded careful and respectful assent with slight reservations. Special notice, of course, was paid to the author's analysis of the role of value systems. One Catholic reviewer felt that Pawełczyńska's analysis offered proof that situational ethics do not suffice for man as a moral code, for if the prisoners had conformed to such a code the Nazi experiment would have succeeded. A Marxist critic, on the other hand, felt that her analysis of value reduction showed how situation ethics could and did function, since the norms created in the camp differed from pre-camp norms.

What these reviews revealed was a curious ambiguity. Pawełczyńska's most significant conclusion is that a deeply internalized value system enabled many prisoners to survive biologically and morally, that is, to resist surrender to violence. Yet the discreetness of her formulation, the cursory characterization of that value system and of its modification under camp conditions, the avoidance of a discussion of the process of its internalization, gave rise to the different interpretations among Polish reviewers. Since she conceived of her study as an "outline" of the problems (as it is subtitled in Polish), one cannot expect fully detailed elaboration. Nevertheless the ambiguity remains. Both Marxist and Catholic critics interpreted her book rather freely in ways that would seem to support their own ideological positions. And yet underlying all the responses was a profound unity of acceptance, though vaguely formulated in terms such as "contribution to present-day humanism," "innovative scholarly reflection," and "important communicational tool for creating a special kind of social awareness."

It is a peculiar circumstance of the Polish edition that only 5000 copies were printed. For a book dedicated to mothers, written in lucid, everyday prose, about a subject of common human interest, one might expect a very large readership. The novelistic *Smoke over Birkenau* by S. Szmaglewska (English translation published in 1947) has appeared in Poland over the last thirty years in half a dozen editions, each averaging some 20,000 copies.

Perhaps this situation is related to Pawełczyńska's observation in the introduction that today's young people should not be compelled to go through the horrors of her generation's experiences; only educators and politicians need be informed in detail on these matters. But paradoxically, the book is admirably suited as an introductory textbook, and the author has taken pains to avoid the specialist vocabulary of her discipline, which suggests that her original intent was to reach a wide readership.

It has been observed by a Polish critic that Pawełczyńska's scholarly study makes "as compelling reading as many an authentic memoir." The author has crafted this effect quite subtly. As her calmly phrased analysis unfolds, it is accompanied by an almost dramatic tension. The straightforward style of the text suits her restrained presentation, but the epigraphs at the head of each chapter carry an intensely emotional and moral loading. The majority are taken from Polish and Western writers, but three are her own, selected from unpublished "desk-drawer" writings. An unorthodox procedure, to be sure, but the epigraphs are in fact a conscious device in the spirit of Bruno Bettelheim's reflection, "No longer can we be satisfied with a life where the heart has its reasons, which reason cannot know. Our hearts must know the world of reason, and reason must be guided by an informed heart."[3] Their function is to indicate the distance between the subjective and objective poles of the intense effort to submit the personal experience of extremity to an impersonal, scientific apparatus. The mottos from non-Polish writers (many from Camus) assert the author's traditional Polish sense of connection with Western, and especially French, values, while the moral stance she adopts in the text as defender of the concepts of the sacredness of the human person and the freedom of the individual suggests a new version of Poland's ancient role as guardian at the ramparts of Western civilization.

Often the writing in the body of the text itself produces a literary effect. For example, long after the last sentences of chapter seven are read, the evocation of a great crime remains in our minds, impressed all the more powerfully by the tension of confinement to homely, material objects—clothing, shoes, children's toys. To charge a few simple sentences with a perception of the "banality of evil" is an economy of expression which merits no little admiration.

Most of the literature on the camps is not found in English.

3. Bruno Bettelheim, *The Informed Heart: Autonomy in a Mass Age* (New York: The Free Press, 1960), p. viii.

Anglophones made up only a small minority in the camps. And, as Pawełczyńska suggests, those who did not experience Nazi terror declined to bang their heads against the wall of misfortune, preferring to protect their optimistic outlooks. An instance in my own life comes to mind: the American author John Steinbeck visited Poland (as part of a cultural exchange) while I was studying there in 1961. Steinbeck was scheduled to visit the Auschwitz Museum, a customary gesture expected of all foreign visitors, but he gruffly refused: "It's like a corpse on the road. I wouldn't stop for it." Many Poles were deeply shocked, as was I, who had become extremely sensitized in the course of my studies to this particular realm of Polish consciousness. Yet Steinbeck's remark activated inner mechanisms in my own psyche: my optimistic American values and my knowledge that Nazi atrocities had all too often been used as a political football by the regime made Steinbeck's blunt pragmatism seem like the healthiest attitude in the face of such horror and evil. And so I, too, turned my back.

Recently there has been a renewal of interest in the experience of the camps, especially (but not only) among the children of survivors (see the *New York Times Magazine*, 19 June 1977). Evidence of this is the increasing demand for college courses in "holocaust literature" throughout North America, the appearance of feature films and documentaries, news articles and TV specials. The upsurge doubtless coincides with a general uneasiness over human survival on this planet in a technological age, reflected in many contemporary literary works. The publication last year of Terrence Des Pres's brilliant study of Nazi and Soviet camps, *The Survivor* (New York: Oxford University Press, 1976), marked a new stage in the assessment of the camps. And now there is Pawełczyńska. It is to be hoped that these authors will be responsible for reversing society's negative view of camp survivors and for inspiring "ultimate concern."

Pawełczyńska and Des Pres argue that negative evaluation of survival behavior in the concentration camp has been the result of erroneous criteria; all the accepted explanations have been based on theories of *civilized* man. Bruno Bettelheim's *The Informed Heart* (Glencoe, Ill.: Free Press, 1960) presents the theory which has perhaps carried the greatest weight among explanations of behavior in the camps. In Bettelheim's view (which he developed in 1943, based on his one-year sojourn at Buchenwald before the war), adaptation to the camp, for the large majority of prisoners, was achieved by means of a regression to childish dependency upon their guards, the SS. The final stage of this adaptation was marked by total identification with the aggressor.

Des Pres and Pawełczyńska are the first to take serious issue with Bettelheim's theory. It is incongruous, they maintain, and an error, to apply psychoanalysis to the camps where material conditions forced prisoners to make a leap out of civilization into humanity's "misty past" and where a totally negative environment was created to transform the prisoners into mindless, predictable, controllable creatures. Nor are crude behaviorist theories relevant to camp behavior, for they begin with the premise that the self is the victim of the environment. Both authors point out the difference between absolute conformity to necessity and strategic conformity to necessity, which provides a convincing counterargument to views of the prisoner as passive victim or tool of terror. In thus rescuing survivors of the camps from the victim-aggressor bind, the authors enable the reader to come away with his or her own humanity—understanding, compassion, moral acuity—intact.

Des Pres elected to explore the "will to live" aspect of survival, frequently mentioned in earlier camp literature. By means of literary analysis which at times attains to poetic insight, and the dubious application of concepts from the biological sciences, he elaborates a not altogether lucid theory of the biological base of human ethics. His theory, as several of his critics have observed, could lead to the notion that physical survival is everything, and it is hard to see that analogies with less complicated organisms can be applied to concentration camp prisoners any more legitimately than psychoanalysis. Pawełczyńska avoids these pitfalls because she does not take her analysis beyond human categories, nor depart from the ethical-sociological plane.

To the younger reader Pawełczyńska's moral judgments on Nazism may seem overstressed, for in the eyes of some the crimes committed by the Allied powers represented on the Nürnberg Tribunal—for example, in Soviet labor camps and during the United States involvement in Vietnam or France's involvement in Algeria—have undermined the moral stature of their judgments. Yet crimes become no less criminal for being approximated or even matched by others. And if in Pawełczyńska's work Nazism is condemned over and over, it must be understood in the context of the writing. Often in Eastern-bloc countries the Nazi era is universalized to the order of a metaphor. Pawełczyńska would not have the reader stop at Nazi Germany; her concern is the protection of human rights in the world *today* and resistance "toward *all* [italics mine] forms of perverted authority that, under the guise of law, perpetrate criminal activity."

But the larger part of her study is taken up with the mechanisms of individual resistance to coercion—the "small, stubborn, and laughable daily heroism in the face of misery." Although her analysis keeps to the moral-social plane and foregoes scrutiny of the origins and formation of those "deeply internalized values" which, she concludes, underlay spontaneous reactions that were conducive to more than individual survival (e.g., cooperation) in the camp—there are signposts in the text pointing to a deeper level. For example, in chapter one she explains that people outside the camp who rendered aid to prisoners did so out of a *"simple response* [italics mine] to a heart that was sensitive to pain and the dimensions of that pain." The epigraphs hint of a personal dimension that cannot be encompassed in the categories of reason alone, for example, Sabato's "not reason . . . will save the world, but *irrational hope* [italics mine] . . . the stubborn will to remain alive." The sentence which ends her study celebrates the new value created by the camps: "a *bond* [italics mine] with the wronged, which demands the greatest sacrifices." If her humanism is to be consistent that bond must be a personal one, not a political slogan. If these concepts—simple response to the heart, irrational hope, bond with the wronged—were investigated further would that search be fulfilled in biology?

In *Emperor of the Earth* (Berkeley and Los Angeles: University of California Press, 1977), a recently published collection of essays by the eminent Polish poet and man of letters, Czesław Miłosz, there are two pieces on the problem of evil—the problem of "Who can justify the suffering of the innocent?" One examines the thought of Russian philosopher Lev Shestov, the other of French philosopher Simone Weil. Both thinkers were antirationalists in the sense that they refused to "rationalize" the problem of evil; acceptance of a world ruled by iron necessity was only possible by means of a leap—of faith.

In his essay on Weil, Miłosz calls attention to her belief that, in spite of the increasing oppression of the individual by collective humanity in technological civilization, "we cannot dismiss history. . . . Willing or not, we are committed. We should throw our act into the balance by siding with the oppressed and by diminishing as much as possible the oppressive power of those who give orders."

Miłosz, who was one of the first to promote the work of Simone Weil with his translation of her selected writings into Polish for publication as an anthology by the journal *Kultura* (Paris, 1958), also explains that he was partially motivated by his resentment of Poland's "division into two camps: clerical and anti-clerical, nationalistic Catholic and Marxist—I exclude of course, the . . . bureaucrats . . . catching every wind from Moscow. I suspect unorthodox Marxists (I use that word for lack of a better one) and non-nationalistic Catholics have very much in common, at least common interests." He notes that Weil was French by nationality, Jewish by descent, agnostic by family upbringing, Catholic by personal affinity.

It seems to me that the author of *Values and Violence* understands the wisdom of Simone Weil, has touched that common ground. And it is in this light, despite ambiguities, that her work should be viewed. If the history of humanity consists, as Pawełczyńska would have it, in a series of oppressions and resistances, if the Nazi years were only the beginning of an era of collective coercion, then it is the ultimate concern of present and future generations to be able to recognize oppression at its earliest indications and be assured of the possibility of resistance.

Catherine S. Leach

Author's Introduction

Plague is not made to man's measure, and so we tell ourselves that plague is unreal—a bad dream that will pass. But the dream does not always pass; it is people who pass, humanists especially, from bad dream to bad dream, for they were not careful enough.

A. Camus, The Plague

T HE WRITING of this book needed the perspective of thirty years. Only historical distance, long reflection, and the calm of approaching old age made it possible to consider the concentration camp in objective categories.

From this perspective Hitler's era stands out not only as traumatic for the prisoners of concentration camps and for the countries occupied by Nazis, but also for the people of Germany, who were perverted by a degenerate system of government.

The fitting of scholarly apparatus to a difficult period of one's biography is no simple task. I have attempted—in as impersonal a way as possible—to select and classify such phenomena and their patterns of connection as will help to make clear the mechanisms by which the concentration camp operated. Here I include not only the mechanisms which gave rise to the specific form the camps took, but also the mechanisms which caused some of the prisoners to survive.

I have tried to approach the subject of Auschwitz with maximum reserve. Its "horrors" I have purposely avoided, because it is my profound conviction that to broadcast naturalistic descriptions of atrocities can be harmful to those fortunate enough never to have met with concentration-camp reality. I have limited my consideration to those mechanisms and elements of the crime which must be known in order to understand how that crime came into being. Simultaneously I wish to present the mechanisms of individual and organized resistance in extremity—the inner resources which man, under extreme conditions, is capable of bringing to bear against crime.

I think it is a mistake to familiarize young people in obsessive detail with the personal biography of our generation. That knowledge is needful for the educator or the politician, who is obliged to keep a constant check on his or her own activity and to foresee its consequences. For educators the knowledge is necessary in order to form, during the educative process, a human person who is capable of recognizing evil—even when its occurrence is still relatively innocent—and of consciously, actively resisting it. For politicians the knowledge is indispensable for exerting a check on their activities and for bringing the understanding that there is no end which justifies every means. Such knowledge is also needed by all those who would guard the world against any breach of human rights.

Nazism as an organized structure has vanished; it was judged by the moral and legal norms operating in our time, within our sphere of civilization. The perpetrators of crimes who did not elude justice's measure were judged with full observance of due process. The court records from the trials of those war criminals arouse in the reader an urge to protest, to rebel. The manner of examining the witnesses (prisoners who survived), of defending the accused, the whole courtroom procedure seems grotesque, if one compares the dimensions of the crime to the legal means at the disposal of the court.[1] And yet it had to be this way. To

1. Kazimierz Kąkol, *Sąd nierychliwy. Frankfurcki proces oprawców z*

apply the rule of "an eye for an eye, a tooth for a tooth"—balancing the punishment in measures of guilt—would have erased the whole meaning of human culture. The world would have been transformed into a never-ending hell of vengeance-seeking.

In the narrow, legal sense, justice was partially dispensed, but ineradicable vestiges of the great crime have remained. These are constantly reactivated in society because there are people alive who survived the camps and people who contributed to their existence. The camps have now entered humanity's history, have become part of the historical consciousness of some of the nations of Europe.

At present we are witnessing important historical events: efforts aimed at transforming Europe into a peace zone. In this struggle for basic human values all those most heavily tried by their experience must strive to break the chain of hatred and revenge in which the modern world has been forged. Such an attitude is very difficult and requires—especially for those whose whole life has been clouded by resentment against that crime—a tremendous mustering of spiritual resources. The struggle for peace and for human values is not waged only in high political circles. On the contrary, that struggle takes place in people's attitudes and is worked out in cooperative efforts.

For example, within the Polish nation, within individual members of that nation, a difficult struggle to change an attitude is going on. But the results will depend, to a large extent, on the kind of attitude that each German will take. The law is but an imperfect system, and even were that system the best possible one, legal norms would never fully coincide with moral norms.

This struggle for solidarity, for society's total condemnation of all war criminals and their ideological heirs, needs to be waged throughout the world. The problem will not be solved by legal statutes, nor even by a formula such as the deprivation of civil

Oświęcimia (Warsaw, 1966); Poland, Główna Komisja Badania Zbrodni Hitlerowskich w Polsce, *Biuletyn*, VII (Warsaw, 1951).

and ceremonial rights; it will take the body of public opinion united in universal condemnation. Those guilty of crimes against humanity deserve civic death, total isolation from society, as the expression of a moral judgment on such crimes and their perpetrators.

In countries not touched by Nazi terror to the degree that Poland was, it is understandable, in a way, that society should shield itself from a knowledge of what took place, and should balk at understanding the circumstances that gave rise to it.

People living within the orbit of European civilization today defend themselves from the naturalistic eloquence of facts which have no analogy in their experience by a failure of the imagination. They resist a phenomenon which cannot be understood or interpreted in any of the accessible social, philosophical, psychological, or moral categories. Such people, as members of that same human species to which the murderers and their victims belong, resist identifying with either murderer or victim. And, lastly, such people protect their view of the world, their optimistic philosophy of life, from the consequences of understanding the concentration camp as a dimension of the evil man can do and of the depth of contempt to which he can sink.

As Antoni Kępiński has said, "The prisoners of Nazi concentration camps are often an enigma to themselves; in any case, they perceive more vividly than other people the enigma of human nature and the illusoriness of human norms, shapes, and appearances. . . . Those who survived a concentration camp often ask themselves: what is this person really like? How would he have behaved in the camp? What would have become of his dignity, righteousness, and so on, if he were to find himself suddenly 'in there'?"[2] The answers to such questions are generally feared; people today do not desire a knowledge of life which compels the asking of such questions.

2. A. Kępiński, "Tzw. KZ-syndrom. Próba syntezy," *Przegląd Lekarski,* no. 1 (1970). [More recently, Kępiński, a Kraków psychiatrist, has published a book-length study of the camps, *Rytm życia (The Rhythm of Life)*, Kraków, 1972.—TRANS.]

It is not true that "suffering ennobles." Suffering can strength-
en, but it can also totally shatter. Life can be lived within the
conventions of decency without banging one's head against the
wall of human misfortunes. But should there arise in a person a
real need for such an understanding, should he be capable of
tearing himself away from normal routine, should he manage to
turn his back on socially sanctioned personal ambitions and
egoisms—he will expose himself to a life considerably more painful but perhaps richer. The understanding of ultimate situations
allows one to look life or death in the eye with courage; it allows
one to view the affairs of men against the background of history.
It also enables one to understand that the ability to inflict terror
and commit crime and the capacity to resist violence have shaped
the history of one generation after another. Only the psychic and
historical manifestations of that resistance are different.

CHAPTER ONE

The World Outside the Camp: Frames of Reference

This especially dangerous segment of the struggle was at the same time a battle for something larger than armed victory; we were fighting for the triumph of humanist values over an inhuman system.
T. Strzembosz, The Rescue of Prisoners in Warsaw, 1939–44

THE STUDY OF Auschwitz as a sociological problem could be restricted, no doubt, to an analysis of a particular, isolated society made up of those subjected to violence and those who generated it. To confine it to that, however, would radically diminish the potential for understanding the social phenomenon of the concentration camp—a phenomenon resisted by the modern Western mind, formed as it is by European humanist culture, the Christian ethic, and the ideals of liberty, equality, and fraternity. Despite the concentration-camp prisoners' isolation from the outside world, that world had a direct and indirect effect on the entire camp system as well as on the various forms of resistance to that system. On the one hand, the outside world acted as a power in complicity with the mechanism of terror—but at the same time it created diverse frames of reference that helped to determine the odds for defense in the broadest meaning of the word.

At least brief reference should be made, therefore, to the set of facts which reveal the essence of Nazi crimes, the apogee of whose expression was Auschwitz, and also to the values of humanism, which, although they underwent modifications in the clash with camp reality, fundamentally affected prisoners' attitudes, behavior, and forms of adaptation. These values affected the manner of experiencing life and death.

The Authority of Terror

My intention was not to write a treatise on the origins of Nazism, its history and social base. There is a very rich literature dealing with these problems, and they are the concern of the specialists researching in various scientific disciplines for theories to explain them. My aim is simply to isolate at least some of the phenomena and some of the patterns that will enable Auschwitz to be seen as an organized structure, and that will illuminate the substance of the protest guiding the activity of the nations that put up a struggle. These phenomena and these patterns shaped the awareness of the prisoners in concentration camps.

Nazism grew up within the framework of a legally functioning German state. This state repeatedly violated the international law[1] of the day, until finally it enriched human culture with a new criminal category: genocide, a crime with which the legal imagination of European civilization had not managed to cope until faced directly with the fact.

It matters little to our subsequent deliberations whether we are dealing with a take-over by a criminal group, or whether the Nazi government, as it consolidated its power, acquired more and more of the characteristics of a criminal organization.[2] In the cases tried in German courts before 1933, the activity of Hitler's storm troopers was construed as criminal.[3] Composed of people

1. Franciszek Ryszka, *Państwo stanu wyjątkowego* (Wrocław, 1964); Andrzej Józef Kamiński, *Faszyzm* (Warsaw, 1971).
2. Alan Bullock, *Hitler: A Study of Tyranny*, rev. ed. (London: Odhams, 1964), Book I.
3. E.g., Rudolf Hoess, *Autobiography* (London: Weidenfeld, 1959). [Hoess was Commandant at Auschwitz; he was tried and hanged by the Poles in 1947.— Trans.]

from the margins of society, these squads posed a threat to fundamental moral and legal norms, and at the time wise individuals realized the danger.[4] To apply the "gang" concept to this era would not wholly contradict the popular view, considering the acknowledged criminal activities and social makeup of the stormtroopers, as well as their intellectual and moral level and the gangsterish methods of dispensing justice within the group.

The situations before and after 1933 differ in these respects: (1) actions previously characterized as criminal grew more and more frequent and more brutal; (2) these actions were committed by members of a group that proved its strength by taking command of the machinery of government, and whose numbers were increasing at a very swift rate and gaining support from a sizable part of society. In that same society the judging of an action as criminal and of its perpetrators as criminals underwent a radical and very speedy change from the moment the perpetrators of those deeds came to power. Deeds recognized before then as criminal were elevated to the rank of universally binding norms.[5] Prohibitions other than those formerly in force were introduced; the substance of moral standards and customs was transformed; the idea of a human person changed; the hierarchy of previously accepted values succumbed to decay.

The Nazi era supplies a great many facts for the interpretation of which the cultural, scientific, and legal concepts operating in the twentieth century do not suffice. Before the year 1933 there existed in German society humanist traditions, for the most part acknowledged everywhere and constituting the common basis of European cultural life: respect for the human person, human life, and justice. There also functioned (to a considerably greater

---

4. Stefan Czarnkowski warned, analyzing these problems: "It's not a question of whether an organized proletariat and the working classes in general would, in favorable circumstances, have the means to oppose and even to paralyze the Fascists' games. They should nevertheless be aware of those games." Stefan Czarnkowski, "Ludzie zbędni w służbie przemocy," in *Dzieła* (Warsaw, 1956), vol. II, p. 193. (An article originally published in 1935.)

5. E.g., the works by A. Bullock, A.J. Kamiński, and R. Hoess, cited above in notes 1, 2 and 3.

degree than in other societies) instrumental values such as order-liness, obedience, economy, frugality, accuracy, and thorough-ness. As a consequence of the situation after 1933, humanist values gradually ceased to operate as the basic frame of reference. Other values were endorsed, such as strength, Germany's supe-riority over other nations, the superiority of the German "race," and the superiority of the strong over the weak. At the same time, rules of conduct that derived from the instrumental values pre-viously operative were given new meaning and made into abso-lutes. From the value of obedience came the imperative to obey Nazi authority blindly; out of the recognition of strength as a value came the imperative to apply strength with brutality. Rec-ognition of national and racial superiority entailed the obligation to exterminate "inferior" races and nations.

German society in large part showed itself capable of accepting these increasingly peremptory imperatives, sanctioned by the power and authority of the state in the name of national megalo-mania. The authority of brute force replaced all moral authorities.

Because of the intense terror employed by the Nazis against the entire society, opposition groups within Germany acting in defense of humanist values did not find in their society the sup-port that would have made possible an effective struggle against the authority of the state. This whole set of circumstances and situations became the cause of Germany's drama, a drama that was played out on various levels and which led—by destroying the solidarity among all formal and informal groups who rejected the Nazi program or methods—to the moral debasement of the society, especially to the moral debasement of the young people who were subjected to the intense activity of Nazi propaganda and Nazi education. As a result there ensued a widespread moral regression within the German nation, which permitted criminal and terrorist activity to take place on the territory of many coun-tries of Europe.

Thus did a powerful criminal gang spring from the bosom of the German people, a gang in which status was assigned accord-ing to degree of participation in making and implementing decisions and in the advantages attained. German society became largely incapable of independent moral reflection; either through apathy or through conscious participation, it came to accept criminal activity, profiting in various ways from the crimes committed in different countries. Such an attitude had little to do with one's place in society and one's level of education.

Common sense is somewhat at odds with the notion that a group that wins power, gains acceptance and cooperation from a significant number of its own people and compels the majority to a blind obedience can be a criminal gang. But substantial data argue in favor of such an interpretation: (1) time after time Nazi activity violated principles of international law, rejecting codes that formed the basis of relations between states; (2) Nazi power was not bound by any rules in relation to the people subject to it; (3) adherents of the Nazi program of genocide erased and destroyed the traces of the crimes they committed, thereby revealing an awareness of the criminal nature of their activity; (4) in occupied countries Nazi activity was unequivocally perceived as criminal activity, contrary to moral law and to what is right; (5) in the minds of concentration-camp prisoners, the system inflicted upon them was unequivocally perceived as an organized, criminal system.

The criminal activity of the Nazi state produced a "German gangster" stereotype in peoples' minds in the occupied countries of Europe—especially in the minds of Poles, who experienced many years of civilian terror and mass-murders. This stereotype into which all Germans were cast contains a moral judgment on directly observed behavior and constitutes a response to the criminal deeds perpetrated systematically throughout the entire period of the occupation.

Defense of the Dimension of Life

The invasion of Poland by the German army as a consequence of the September 1939 Blitzkrieg marked the beginning of many years of misfortune for the whole country, and at the same time signalled the start of a great national mobilization. The first reaction to those events was above all patriotic; it was the response of a nation whose elder generation still lived with the memory of the partitions[6] of Poland and whose younger generation knew those times from their parents' firsthand accounts. This new loss of independence was taken as a tragic continuation of Poland's history; at the same time, the historical bond drew both generations closer to the models and values of their forefathers' battle for independence.

The very first period of the occupation and the methods of operation it revealed led the Poles to equate their attitude of hostility toward Germans with hostility toward Nazism. What came to be called the "Nazi occupation" passed into history under that name. This obviously does not mean a lessening of patriotic motives; it means that the national struggle was inseparably linked with the struggle to defend basic human values.

A very strong sense of community established itself, which enabled the whole nation to rally around patriotic and moral values. Such a situation made it impossible to form a collaborationist government in Poland, since every form of collaboration met with severe condemnation from a society that was united. Regardless of the differences which divided the groupings of the Polish Underground,[7] whenever it came to the basic issue—their attitude toward Nazism—differences ceased to exist.

The concentration-camp prisoner, even though Nazi terror isolated him in a society deprived of any sort of laws, was at the same time a member of a society that resisted the terror with every means possible in the situation. It was precisely in the sphere of humanist values—from which stemmed the norm of loyally rendering aid to those worse off—that an unbreakable

6. Poland's territory was divided up and annexed three times by Russia, Prussia, and Austria, once in 1772, again in 1793, and again in 1795 when Poland ceased to exist as an independent state. The country did not regain its independence until 1918–19.—TRANS.

7. The groups that were formed to conduct underground activities during the Nazi occupation of Poland numbered some 600.—TRANS.

bond existed between prisoners (especially political prisoners) and their struggling nation. Every show of aid counteracted the prisoners' isolation, which formed a necessary part of the Nazi plan of extermination. The need to minister to those in prison broke every ideological barrier and created a platform for organized cooperation between the various groups of the Polish Resistance. Those who took part in relief actions—underground organizations, families and friends of prisoners, local residents in the vicinity of camps situated on Polish territory—were people not indifferent to misfortune, who risked their lives neither for fame nor reward but in simple response to a heart that was sensitive to pain and the dimensions of that pain. A broadly-based moral community grew up, bringing together people of various social strata, people in various life situations; the awareness of this community constituted a great strength which made it possible for prisoners to mobilize various defense mechanisms to resist Nazi terror. Regardless of what form the relief actually took— from gestures of friendly greeting to aid in organizing escapes— every bit of help from the outside bolstered not only the physical stamina of a concrete individual, but helped many prisoners to muster their psychic forces, something that would have been beyond the means of a person deprived of hope and support.

On both sides of the barbed wire there were people who thought and felt the same, united by a bond of feeling and a hope for the victory of basic human values over the moral depravity represented by the Nazi system.

Tomasz Strzembosz has described the reactions of those who felt that a prisoner condemned to torture and death was still a living human being to be rescued at the risk of one's own life:

The rescue and freeing of prisoners,[8] apart from the immediate and specific meaning it had in the struggle conducted by the Polish Underground with the Nazi occupier, possessed immeasurable moral and

8. During the Nazi occupation Poland had the most powerful resistance movement, operating with the support of nearly the entire society. The rescue of prisoners was carried on throughout the whole period of the occupation in spite of the terror, which was considerably more intense and more widespread than in other occupied countries in Europe.

emotional significance. At every step we encountered German brutality and very likely one could not have found an area of life where its use was not in evidence, but it had the most terrible repercussions of all upon the destinies of those who, as political prisoners, found themselves in the hands of the Gestapo—the Nazi security police. In the minds of every Varsovian, Szucha and Pawiak[9] were terrifying images to which little else could compare. Whoever landed in these prisons had a very slim chance of coming out alive; and it was not only death that awaited them. The system of torture applied in prisons and camps embraced such inhuman physical and spiritual suffering that the accounts which reached us from there surpassed ordinary human understanding. In the face of such tortures, a vial of poison was salvation, death an act of mercy. Even the sight of a Gestapo uniform provoked universal dread, a dread so powerful and so deeply rooted that it was relived over and over, even many years after the war. No wonder then, that each time someone was snatched by force of arms from a fate of torture at German hands, it was experienced not only as an act of long-sought revenge but also as a great solace. Every one of such rescues reduced the number of the tortured, returned to life those who had departed for good—so everyone thought—and strengthened the hope that even from the depths of such hells there was a way out. To this day the soldiers whose lot it was to take part in such missions say that no other armed action ever provided such great satisfaction; nothing could match it. Indeed, in those days there was perhaps no greater gift that one human being could offer another, and it was a gift not only to the imprisoned and tortured, but also to their mothers, wives, children, to everyone close to them, to the whole Warsaw community. The beauty of those deeds was greater than the beauty of the physician's art that brought the dying back to life. How close it was to the laying down of one's life for another. How many obstacles had to be overcome to turn the "almost impossible" into the possible. Today it is hard to imagine how much effort all of this required, how much the decision alone cost us—there was not only the danger of losing, but also of a future bloody reprisal, in just one victory or out-smarting of the enemy. No one ever knew the price that might have to be paid for such an act of friendship, of solidarity, of duty, and many a time we paid very dearly. Yet this, too, was taken into account.[10]

9. Szucha and Pawiak were the chief prisons used for interrogation by the Nazi security police. Szucha, located in the Gestapo headquarters itself, was used solely for torture; Pawiak released prisoners only to be killed or transported to concentration camps (about 60,000 were killed, 30,000 transported to the camps). The Nazis destroyed Pawiak in 1944.—TRANS.

10. Tomasz Strzembosz, *Odbijanie więźniów w Warszawie 1939-1944* (Warsaw, 1972).

Strzembosz's book tells the story of only one segment of the struggle as it was waged in Warsaw. Every camp, every prison in Poland was surrounded by a similar atmosphere of fraternal support. No matter how—given the circumstances under Nazi terror—that support might be actualized, the very awareness that it existed had incommensurable moral and emotional consequences both for prisoners and outside supporters. In conditions of utter hopelessness, hope flickered and grew stronger with every act of opposition, even the smallest, that shattered the terror.

Prices for those acts of friendship and loyalty were paid on both sides of the barbed wire; both the givers and the receivers perished in Nazi reprisals. Every attempt to give aid, even if carried out in hopeless circumstances, and even if it caused heavy losses of life, passed into the legends of camp and prison. In the midst of a world of crime, a world of solidarity came into being, strengthening the attitudes of the unsubmissive, those capable of struggle in the worst conditions. Life, dehumanized by the camp system, acquired new dimensions for the prisoner. A flicker of hope in one's own biological survival appeared, along with the profound faith that out of the struggle then taking place must come the triumph of those values in whose hierarchy the greatest good is the human person.

CHAPTER TWO

Institutions of State Crime

> *Come awake, all of you murderers, living and dead, to an
> eternity of kindness. So that over and over every death camp
> may break your hearts with each person's dying, so that every
> crime may snatch each person's life from your grasp, so that
> every torture inflicted may wound your hearts with each person's
> suffering. So that every abused body may be the body of the
> person dearest to you. May you be every father and every
> mother, and from the depths of a human heart may you feel
> every death as if it were the death of your own children.*
>
> *And let there be no more judgments upon you, divine or human.
> Descend into the hell of memory. Love-stricken forever—keep
> humanity from every crime.*
>
> *A. P.*

CONCENTRATION CAMPS were state institutions of
the Third Reich, operating on the basis of official statutes and a set of strictly secret directives that were
binding on the subordinate levels of government, which acknowledged the right of higher authorities to issue orders and make
laws of this type.[1]

According to historical documents that have been collected
and described, the tasks entrusted by the state to paid personnel
in a concentration camp can be defined as the following:

1. Prisoners sent to a camp are intended to die (no obligation
to justify their deaths) after preliminary exploitation as a work

1. Poland, Główna Komisja Badania Zbrodni Hitlerowskich w Polsce, *Biuletyny*; Państwowe Muzeum w Oświęcimiu, *Zeszyty Oświęcimskie*, and Rudolf
Hoess, *Autobiography* (London: Weidenfeld, 1959).

force performing unskilled manual labor (slave labor, unpaid and unregulated by any legislation).

2. Death should be dispensed in various ways:

a. on a mass scale—through living conditions affording an average chance of survival of up to three months,

b. on a mass scale—through the systematic putting to death of categories of the population viewed as racially inferior,

c. on a mass scale—through the process of selecting for death those unable to work,

d. individually—through the killing of persons designated for "special treatment,"

e. individually—through the killing of random persons by random methods.

3. The question of whom to kill in what order is decided by the paid employees of the camp (or persons deputized by those employees) within a framework of general (constantly changing) directives, e.g., persons unable to work, the sick, the elderly, children, pregnant women, persons of specified nationality, e.g., Jews, Gypsies, Poles, Russians, persons belonging to the intelligentsia (e.g., professors, clergymen).

4. Slave labor should be economically purposeful, but in the event of a dearth of purposeful tasks, labor should be performed for its own sake (utterly senseless hard labor) as one of the methods of diminishing, with time, a prisoner's chances of survival.

5. The totality of living conditions—the food, the hours and conditions of sleep, the hours and conditions of work, lack of health care, lack of elementary hygiene, the way the power structure is organized, the routine duties of a prisoner, the roll calls, the creation of an environment in which epidemics and various diseases spread—serves to reduce the chances of survival.

6. Randomly selected prisoners are treated as test material (for pseudomedical experiments),[2] without regard to the physical and mental effects or the risk to life.

2. For example, prisoners were used to test substances which would ultimately

7. Given the availability of prisoners as test subjects, experimentation with sterilization methods is especially recommended; the results can be applied in long-range planning on a mass scale for the purpose of exploiting the labor of non-German peoples with the assurance that the people of these nationalities will die without offspring.

8. Free labor is supplied to the factories of the Third Reich through a unique kind of slave trade.

9. A new branch of industry arises in which the human body is treated as raw material to be processed.[3]

10. Social engineering prevails: applied stimuli are intended to corrupt the prisoner and to render him useful as an instrument of terror.

11. The plundering, including the sorting, storage, and shipping, of the personal effects of living and dead prisoners is established as a system.

12. A penal system is obligatory for dealing with prisoner behavior meant to postpone death; each employee of the camp, or each person deputized by an employee, is authorized to establish whether such behavior has actually taken place and what penalty to impose.

13. Owing to the secret nature of the majority of directives, concentration-camp personnel are obliged to falsify general reports and the records pertaining to the causes of prisoners' deaths.

---

serve the purposes of the military or the police (e.g., to expose army deserters, to coerce prisoners to confess or to divulge military secrets). Some "prisoner-specimens" were killed with injections of phenol so that autopsies could be performed immediately. Some were killed sadistically with various poisons. Some were frozen to death. Other experiments were conducted to serve the criminal ends of the Nazi government (e.g., experiments on twins for the purpose of discovering a method for faster multiplication of the "superior" German race combined with experiments in sterilization, castration, etc. of "inferior" races). —Trans.

3. After having been exploited for their labor while alive, the bodies of dead prisoners and the victims of the gas chambers provided hair for weaving cloth, gold was salvaged from their teeth, and their ashes served as an ingredient in the manufacture of soap.—Trans.

14. Owing to the secret nature of the activity carried on, concentration-camp personnel are obliged to erase the traces of such activity and to preserve official secrecy.

15. For efficiently performing the tasks necessary to accomplish the above-outlined program and for showing creative initiative in the area of methods, camp personnel are entitled to the following rewards:

    a. advancement in the official hierarchy,
    b. state decorations, bonuses,
    c. additional holidays,
    d. extra rations of food and alcohol.

Duty assignments in concentration camps—like membership in the Nazi party—were voluntary. Only toward the end of the war were there some cases of compulsory assignments to Auschwitz. The SS functionaries undertaking work in a concentration camp were made familiar with the full set of duties which their employment entailed and with the program of activity carried out in the camp.

Analyzing the motives and rationalizations which must have accompanied participation in this program of genocide, and the viewing of it as a career occupation, one can distinguish several basic motivational patterns:

1. Recognition of the Third Reich as a legitimate state and the right of superiors to issue orders led to the acceptance of assignments fulfilled in Auschwitz because the moral and legal authority of the state was viewed as supreme. This interpretation led to the carrying out of entrusted tasks with scrupulous discipline and conscientiousness and to enjoyment of privileges only within the bounds set by regulation.

2. The recognition of the invincible strength of the Third Reich and the acceptance of force as supreme authority—this view brings out a tendency to identify with the aggressor, leads to a conscious striving for personal advancement and to participation in the accepted activity at the highest possible official level. Such

motives led not only to the fulfilling of entrusted tasks, but additionally to the exercise of one's own initiative. An attitude of this sort inclined the functionary to take advantage of privileges either within the bounds established by regulation or outside of those bounds, all the while maintaining caution and restraint lest excesses diminish one's opportunities.

3. Acceptance of the job itself in Auschwitz for its special advantages—it was a shelter from military service at the front; it was secure; for those who stuck to the rules it furnished a large number of opportunities; for those who did not, it provided the chance to thieve on a grand scale and, thanks to this, a life that was alluring while on the job plus considerable material resources for the future. Such a motivational pattern arose out of the need for physical security (an escape from the danger threatening combatants) and the ambition to acquire the greatest number of material goods, assuring a prosperous and comfortable life in the future.

4. Acceptance of a job in Auschwitz as especially alluring because it satisfied a need for daily experiencing one's own dominance and strength, the right to decide life and death, the right to dispense death personally and at random and the right to abuse one's power over the prisoners, even in relation to the limits prescribed by regulation and camp custom—this attitude often went together with alcoholism, sexual deviancy, and a scale of degeneracy that ran considerably higher than in other categories of SS officials.

The above classification of motivational patterns and concomitant attitudes and behavior is not meant to show that all SS functionaries can be divided up on this basis unequivocally; it presumes only that as we analyze this collectivity, we encounter types who come closest to one of the above-mentioned categories.

Many factors determined the possibility of taking up work in a concentration camp of the Auschwitz type. Not every German who recognized the Third Reich as a legitimate power was capable of fulfilling the tasks required of camp personnel. A unique negative selection process must have governed the choice of staff for a concentration camp—a choice of people such as would guarantee their active participation in the carrying out of the various methods of genocide.

It would be quite an oversimplification to state that such a selection was made from among the most depraved criminal elements—although this was certainly the resource for a part of the camp personnel.

The SS functionaries employed in the camp were recruited from various social milieus and, on close examination, can be seen to have reflected a cross-section of society. Although persons from the lower classes with lesser education predominated, we also encounter among the SS in Auschwitz, and among persons who worked closely with them, people who rank very high on the level of education and training (e.g., doctors, school teachers, and even university professors).

The formulation, "negative selection," is based on the fact that a position of this type could be filled by individuals who, as a result of Nazi training, had succumbed to moral degeneracy (in the sense of a deadening of the fundamental moral norms binding in traditional European culture) and by individuals who, in the course of their encounter with camp reality, succumbed to further debasement. This debasement affected various spheres of human response. It led to:

1. Intensification or rapid development of sadistic, psychopathic, and sociopathic traits (disappearance of emotional reactions).

2. Cognitive disturbances—the ability to make independent value judgments totally disappeared; the fundamental concept of "a human person" became twisted, and this had enormous consequences; the categories of person and non-person coincided with German and non-German respectively. In this connection, the beings to be murdered constituted in the killers' minds something like beasts for slaughter—except that slaughterhouses, as

institutions with long traditions, observed regulations concerning humanitarian methods of killing.

3. Disturbances in the area of interpersonal relations in one's own group (a brutal struggle for a higher place in the official hierarchy and for access to higher incomes, denunciations, brutal retaliatory deeds among members of the SS group, mutual distrust, etc.).

4. Thirst for self-enrichment to be gotten by every available method, hence the search for greater opportunities to divide up the loot obtained from the theft of prisoners' effects.

5. The acceptance of an industry for which the bodies of murdered human beings supplied the raw material.

The whole range of actions covered by overt as well as strictly secret directives was performed under the terms of a work agreement. These actions, defined later by the International Tribunal as crimes of genocide, were—according to decisions made at the time by the government of the Third Reich and by various other organs of government, including those in Auschwitz—worthy of the stamp of approval.[4]

There was very little chance that a camp employee acting under Nazi orders could commit deeds which could be prosecuted as crimes. The crimes against life were never construed as felonious, regardless of whether they were an essential part of the machinery of mass murder, the result of personal initiative in the area of victimizing individuals, or a form of sophisticated play which consisted of devising extra torments and new ways of killing. This type of activity was covered by a system of rewards.

On the whole, small-scale looting of property was not prosecuted. In principle, effects were to be duly handed over to the treasury of the Third Reich. However, owing to the strictly secret

4. Tadeusz Cyprian and Jerzy Sawicki, "Oświęcim w procesie norymberskim," *Warmia, Mazury*, no. 2 (1962); Tadeusz Hołuj, "Auschwitz-proces kryminalny," *Polityka*, no. 35 (1965) and "Uwagi o procesie frankfurckim," *Życie Literackie*, no. 4 (1960).

nature of these activities, various levels of power shared in the apportionment of effects—from SS camp personnel all the way up to their superiors. In these circumstances, penalties for crimes against property were imposed rather sporadically and only upon those SS officials who did not belong to the powerful in-group or who, as a result of denunciations arising out of conflicts over the distribution of loot or because of other conflicts within their own group, were accused of stealing.

It was a punishable and prosecuted offense to "stain the purity of the race" (which meant to produce offspring with a specimen of "inferior race," or to maintain a permanent relationship with such a specimen). To be accused of such a crime, however, one had to have been denounced by one's colleagues in the SS.

Criminal prosecution of any deed committed by an SS functionary employed in Auschwitz was determined above all, therefore, by conflicts, antagonisms, rivalries, and the disparate interests within the SS.

If we treat the SS functionaries employed in a concentration camp as one limb of a wide-branching and hierarchical criminal group that was perpetrating the crime of genocide and utilizing living persons for pseudomedical experimentation and the bodies of the murdered for industrial purposes, that was profiting from slave labor and stolen property, that was torturing people by nearly every possible method, it must be clearly emphasized that every successively higher link in the chain of command, up to the top leadership of the Nazi party and government, was part of that group responsible for these crimes and that this group included numerous tycoons of industry and their subsidiary organizations, as well as some members of the health-care field. Besides this, some parts of German society at large performed functions which contributed to the existence and operation of concentration camps, and some consciously enjoyed advantages from the continuous criminal activity carried on in the camps.

A special feature of this gang was that, demoralized by its increasingly brutal criminal behavior, it disintegrated from within. The moral norms that generally exist in criminal groups, but apply only to their members, gradually broke down. Instead of the signs of solidarity, a power struggle and internal conflicts of interest took over.

The secret and anonymous character of the majority of decisions, as well as the effort to cover up this activity, is evidence that many of the participants knew their actions to be criminal. Such tendencies are observable from the highest down to the lowest levels of government, the party, and business.

CHAPTER THREE

Living Space

> A tranquility so peaceful and so indifferent seemed to cancel
> out almost effortlessly the old images of the plague: Athens
> reeking of pestilence, forsaken even by the birds, Chinese cities
> filled with the death agony of silent victims, the convicts of
> Marseilles piling oozing corpses into pits, the building of a
> great wall in Provence to check the raging wind of pestilence,
> Jaffa and its hideous beggars, the damp and putrefying mat-
> tresses stuck to the dirt floor in the hospital at Constantinople,
> where the sick were dragged by hooks, the masked carnival
> of doctors during the Black Death, copulation of the living
> in the cemeteries of Milan, cartloads of corpses in terrified
> London, and an endless human scream filling the nights and
> days, everywhere, always.
>
> *A. Camus*, The Plague

T HE SITE at Auschwitz [Oświęcim], where from 1941 to 1945 the *Konzentrationslager Auschwitz-Birkenau* [Oświęcim-Brzezinka] was located, has now become a museum of martyrology and a reserve of documents. The museum is actually housed in the original camp (Auschwitz I). The premises of the museum, Auschwitz-Birkenau (Auschwitz II), consist of a quiet stretch of land, lush and green, on which stand primitive huts and buildings.

A person who strays here by accident cannot even guess that within this small area all the varieties of human crime, and all the conceivable dramas, misfortunes, sufferings, and humiliations that ever happened in different corners of the globe and in different epochs of history were perpetuated—that on this piece of land, crimes took place such as the history of humankind had never known.

This modest site is the largest cemetery in the world and there is no way of accurately recreating the number of the slain and the tortured. According to very uncertain and incomplete data, at least 4,000,000 people were gassed in Auschwitz. There were around 405,000 officially registered prisoners in Auschwitz; [in the general category were] 202,000 men and around 89,000 women; [in special categories were] about 20,000 Gypsies and over 13,000 Russian prisoners of war. In separately numbered series (A & B), over 60,000 Jews were registered, and over 12,000 prisoners sent "for correction" with a specific time-limit on their sojourn.[1] In addition there were great numbers of unregistered prisoners from Silesia [Śląsk].[2]

At Home

The site of Auschwitz is a cemetery where the remains of millions of people from all over Europe are buried. Before this happened, the people dwelled on the site which defined the spatial limits of their shorter or longer lives. The site of Auschwitz I was contained within bounds of 300 x 200 m. [approx. 1000 ft. x 650 ft.]; the territory of the entire camp of Auschwitz II-Birkenau measured 750 x 1800 m. [approx. 2500 ft. x 6000 ft.] and of this total area, the women's camp (BIa and BIb) occupied a combined site totalling 750 x 300 m. [approx. 2500 ft. x 1000 ft.] in area. (See figures 1 and 2.)

Auschwitz is situated to the west of Kraków on the Soła River in a malarial locale whose severe climate is marked by drastic

1. The camp records were partially destroyed; thus the figures mentioned do not add up to the approximate total of registered prisoners. Nazi officials classified prisoners into different "ideological" categories. This was reflected in the different numerical series under which prisoners were registered: there was a general series for men and women of various nationalities who were neither Jews, nor Gypsies, nor Russian POWs; a separate series (*A & B*) for Jews, both men and women; a separate *Z* series for Gypsy men and women; a separate *R* series for Russian POWs; a separate *E* series for prisoners sent to camp for correction (fugitives from forced labor in the Reich). See Poland, Główna Komisja Badania Zbrodni Hitlerowskich w Polsce, *Biuletyn*, I (Warsaw, 1946) p. 83 —Trans.

2. Ludwik Rajewski, *Oświęcim w systemie RSHA* (Warsaw-Kraków, 1946).

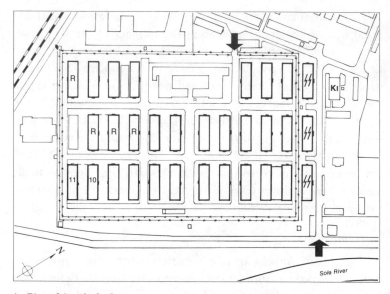

1. Plan of Auschwitz I.
   K: Crematory I; R: camp hospital barracks; 10: barracks where pseudo-medical experiments were conducted; 11: "death barracks." The rest of the barracks inside the barbed wire were prisoners' residences.

changes of temperature. The camp was divided into many parts located at some distance from Auschwitz and from Birkenau (see maps). Auschwitz I was a show camp; it contained 28 brick buildings, 20 of which were residential; it was appointed with a hospital and two bathhouses. In the initial phase of construction the prisoners slept on the floor; later they built three-tiered bunks.

Auschwitz II, the largest part of the camp, consisted of six sections designated by the letters *a* to *f*. These sections were cut off from each other by electrically-charged barbed wire fences. A second barrier of barbed wire surrounded the camp as a whole. Besides the wire to insure against escapes, a line of armed sentries, constantly on the watch from wooden towers, ringed the sections. A second line of watches was stationed at a distance further removed. The men's sections contained wooden barracks

2. Plan of Auschwitz II—Birkenau.

1 and 2: The women's camp. 3: Men's quarantine camp. 4: Family camp for Czech Jews. 5 and 6: The men's camp. 7: Family camp for Gypsies. 8: Hospital in men's camp. 9: Under construction; known as "Mexico." 10: Storehouses of plundered effects; known as "Canada." K: Crematories and gas chambers. 11: Rail platform; site of "selections" for gas chamber. R: Hospital barracks in women's camp. W1: Kitchens. W2: Bathhouses; place to get water in women's camp. U: Washrooms and toilets without running water. Continuous lines around sections = electrically charged barbed wire.

whose construction had been adapted from stables; the women's section consisted partly of brick buildings and partly of wooden barracks adapted from stables. The camp in Birkenau [Brzezinka] and, therefore, the women's camp too, was erected on swampy ground. The mud on which the barracks were built never dried. Both BIa and BIb sections contained about sixty buildings. The stable-like wooden barracks were devoid of windows; the so-called brick buildings were one-story shacks with eight sealed windows, measuring 1 sq. meter [about 3 sq. ft.] in area, and one stove. Both wooden and brick structures were set directly on the clay soil without a vapor barrier. Air penetrated the buildings through numerous chinks. In the brick barracks, four *Stuben* [rooms] were marked off; between the partition walls, which were 230 cm. high [about 7½ ft.], two wooden decks measuring 170 cm. x 200 cm. [about 5½ x 6½ ft.], were fastened horizontally at a height of 75 cm. [less than 2½ ft.] from each other, above a brick floor. These three horizontal layers (including the lowest, which was part of the brick floor) were called "roosts"; each of them was a refuge and a bedroom for 5 to 12 women, depending on congestion in the camp. The barracks, depending on that congestion, were intended to shelter 600 to 800, often 1000 to 1400, women.

The wooden barracks were furnished with three-tiered, single (as a rule) bunks measuring approximately 100 x 175 cm. [3¼ ft. x 5¾ ft.] on which several women slept. (See figures 3 and 4.) The so-called hospital barracks had bunk beds of the same dimensions. Women who were gravely ill would lie naked, 4 at a time, on the bare planks or on thin, rotting straw mattresses, covered by one lice-infested blanket. Each of these buildings, intended for 200 occupants, had to make room for around 700 women, even though the basis for admittance was a fever of over 39° Celsius [about 103°F].

The ground in front of the barracks was used for the morning and evening roll calls (lasting many hours) and for the dispensing of food rations (one-half litre [about 1 pt.] of liquid, morning and

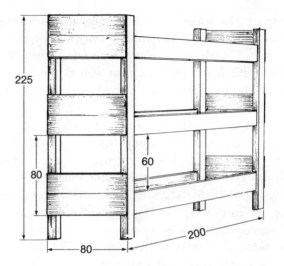

3. Dimensions of bunk beds (in cm.).

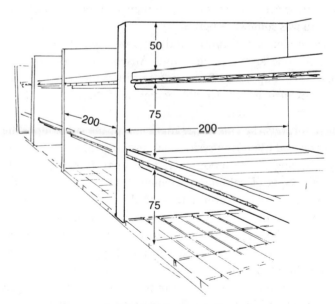

4. Dimensions of roosts (in cm.).

evening, about 200 grams [7 oz.] of bread, sometimes with a piece of margarine or other accompaniment); three-quarters of a litre [1½ pt.] of rutabaga or nettle soup was dispensed to the work crews in the field. The space, as well as the food rations intended for the prisoners, was shared with ever-multiplying hordes of rats and trillions of insects.

The women's camp had two temporary washrooms, each of which held about forty persons, but they were closed, as a rule, to most of the prisoners. They were used chiefly by prisoner-functionaries. The opening of the washrooms was certain to trigger a brutal battle for access to water. The *Zauna*, or camp bathhouse, served the *Zugänge* for their minute-long bath, and only in so-called "delousing" operations did women prisoners from all disinfected sections of the camp walk through it. Toilets were equally inaccessible and unsuitable for coping with the numbers of prisoners, and the concept of "hygienic conditions" is totally useless for evaluating them.

In this respect the situation in the men's camp at Auschwitz II-Birkenau was somewhat better.

The remainder of the camp landscape was completed by five crematories—one at the main camp (Auschwitz I) and four at Birkenau. (See map 2 and figure 5.) At full capacity the crematories could burn about 10,000 bodies in a twenty-four hour period.

If one interprets the site of the main camp, the subcamps, the construction and use of the residential dwellings in spatial terms, then considering the function served an analogy can be made with certain types of colonial settlements. The subcamps numbered, on the average, several tens of thousands of prisoners; they formed peculiar city-states set apart by boundaries, the crossing of which was prohibited to their inhabitants and carried penalties similar to those attached to an illegal crossing of national boundaries. At the same time the communities thus set apart did not comprise distinct groups; they were united by a common bond of similar experiences, similar conditions, and

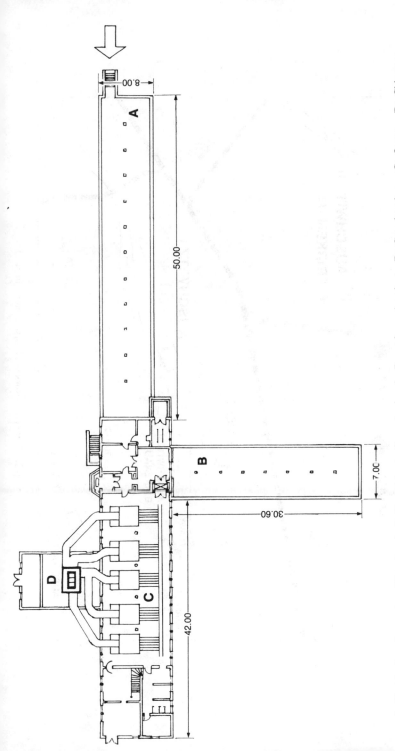

5. Sketch plan of crematory III in Auschwitz II—Birkenau (in meters).   A: Room for undressing.   B: Gas chamber.   C: Ovens.   D: Chimneys.

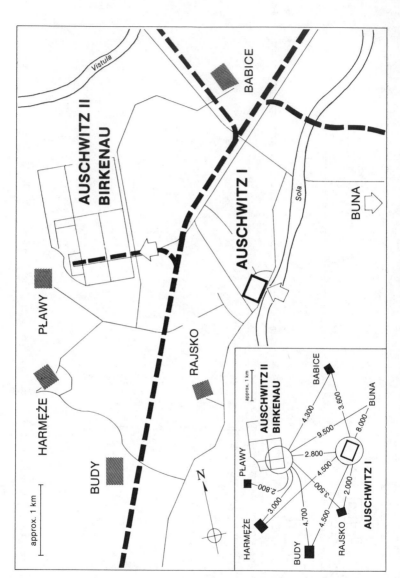

Map 2. Distances to work sites outside camp (in km.).

common goals. These communities had been administratively cut up by the camp authorities for the purpose of impeding any sort of associative activity among people—this prevented the building of an exceedingly numerous community whose united resistance might have been dangerous for the terrorist power structure. The administration of every one of these city-states was based on identical regulations and directives and on the same organization of power. If any differences were apparent, they were due to the individual characteristics of the representatives of camp authority and to the proportional mix of certain categories of prisoners, with the resultant capacity for lesser or greater unity and cooperation.

These administrative divisions did not respect the essential distinctions between prisoners (e.g., nationality, political ideology, criminal record), quite the opposite—one way to guarantee the success of the program of terror was to create conflict-ridden communities, culturally and linguistically disparate, communities in which various sorts of antagonisms had the chance to show up.

Similar principles guided the assignment of prisoners to living quarters; there was deliberate avoidance of a system of quartering that would permit segregation into homogeneous groups of one nationality or homogeneous groups of political prisoners. In the few cases where this principle was ignored, the relative homogeneity of the prisoners was offset by assigning the functions of *Blockältester* to those types of prisoners who would insure the terror by intensifying conflicts and contradictory interests.

The only space that gave one a chance to choose a homogeneous group were the bunk-beds—at best a set of bunks. The sole possibility of consolidating informal groups within the structure of the camp city-state was if a group of prisoners of the same nationality, brought to the camp from the same prison, managed to take over a set of neighboring bunks. The common sleeping space functioned as a home and family as long as it could be protected from the quartering of strangers.

This very limited possibility of creating a spatial base of solidarity, mutual aid, and support was systematically destroyed by the system of transfers to other barracks; in this way informal groups were continuously broken up, but they renewed themselves in each reallocated space.

The territory between barracks functioned as a communication line (much more so than the main street of the camp, where it was easy to meet dangerous camp authorities) between prisoners from various barracks linked by ties of friendship and "business." The ban against entering other barracks than one's own would be circumvented in various ways, or else an information system and meeting place would be set up between the barracks. It was much more difficult to make contact between the separate sections within the same subcamp (in the women's subcamp at Birkenau a gate that was usually guarded by prisoner-functionaries separated fields *a* and *b*). Passing through the gate was associated with a certain risk and required quick wits or factual arguments. The only legal place to meet was at the camp toilets and washrooms—a gathering there was justified by waiting in line.

After being split up by a transfer to different barracks, the informal groups of prisoners sought ways to keep in touch with each other; thus communication arteries and the extremely primitive arrangements serving as washrooms and toilets performed an essential function in the system of prisoner contacts. Other service buildings could not perform this function to the same degree; for example, prisoners sent to the kitchen for food from various barracks could meet with their friends from other barracks only by accident. The *Zauna* (bathhouse) was a place where prisoner groups were taken separately and under close supervision. All storehouses of food and clothing were inaccessible to the vast majority of prisoners. Beside the barbed wire enclosing the women's subcamp at Birkenau ran a narrow strip of bare, muddy ground called—for some unknown reason—"the meadow"; it was a place of meeting and of relative rest during the infrequent intervals between compulsory, regulation activities; it was also the place to which prisoners were forcefully driven from their barracks during non-working hours, and the place to which they were herded naked for "delousing." Depending on the current situation in the camp and on the weather, this same spot could function as the place where prisoners living in different barracks could contact each other (especially on non-working days). During extremely bad weather, when orders were given to forbid entrance to the barracks, it was a place of additional torment.

On one side of the women's subcamp, a railroad platform between two rows of barbed wire separated it from one of the sections of the men's subcamp. During periods of relaxed supervision people could meet their loved ones at this spot, letting themselves be seen, and in this way telling them that they were still alive.

Prisoner communication inside the separate city-states of the camp was often interrupted by so-called *Blocksperre*, a ban for various periods of time against leaving one's own barracks. *Blocksperre* sometimes functioned as a collective punishment, but more often it marked exceptionally ominous events in the life of the camp community (e.g., selection for the gas chamber) or for the life of a several-thousand-member transport which had arrived for gassing. Despite very severe penalties and supervision, *Blocksperre* never prevented some group of prisoners or other from breaking the ban for the purpose of gaining information on the nature of the threat; such reconnaissance produced at least a faint chance of self-defense or mental preparedness for the anticipated threat. Thanks to the breaking of *Blocksperre*, the mass of prisoners was usually informed about the approximate numbers and destinies of the transport herded to the gas chambers. More detailed information was obtained in other ways.

The Road to Work

A good part of the barracks and huts located in the several sections of the subcamp at Birkenau functioned as work areas for prisoner crews utilized inside the grounds of the camp. To be assigned to these sites was every prisoner's dream. Prisoner crews

Auschwitz barracks in winter. Auschwitz Museum archives no. 513.

Close up of Auschwitz barracks. Auschwitz Museum archives no. 3932.

Bunk beds. Auschwitz Museum archives no. 19617

were put to work—among other places inside the camp—in the kitchens, the potato storehouses, the clothing depositories, the laundries, the package depot, the hospitals, in the food supply warehouse, in camp administrative offices, in the bathhouse, and in the canteen. Camp crews also carried out disinfection; they serviced the pumps, toiled at cleanup operations, worked as chimney sweeps, carpenters, electricians, etc. (The barracks' staff, being a part of the camp power-structure, constituted a separate work division). These work crews afforded notably greater chances for survival, especially if the type of work enabled one to supply oneself with extra food and clothing. Even the crews whose situation did not furnish such possibilities at least enabled one to avoid the rain, snow and cold, the long and difficult road to work, and other circumstances that went together with the assignment to random work crews (*Aussenkommandos*) leaving the camp daily to go to work. The permanent work locations and relatively permanent personnel of these crews favored

Bunk beds. Auschwitz Museum archives no. 3812.

Roosts. Auschwitz Museum archives no. 20740/1.

Main entrance to Auschwitz I, with inscription, *Arbeit macht frei*. Auschwitz Museum archives no. 872.

the establishment of informal working groups of prisoners. These groups were a good deal more stable than the familial groups sleeping on one "roost." The core of these groups lasted unchanged for quite a while—the only ones to leave were the sick, the dead, and those dismissed as a punishment for transgressing camp regulations. The relative organization and solidarity of at least a part of the crews, and a common "eye" kept on those in authority, significantly restricted the possibilities of being exposed for offenses against camp regulations.

The work sites, besides consolidating the work crew, performed still another function (thanks to the prisoners' heightened ingenuity) which had nothing to do with the work performed. All cracks and holes, sometimes even larger hiding-places, could serve to keep various necessaries with which prisoners could increase their chances of survival (e.g., food, clothing, medicine) and the crews' occupational contacts constituted a communication network used for transmitting these things to other prisoners, or for exchange. Things connected with the organized resistance movement in the camp could also be kept in these hiding-places.

Field crews (*Aussenkommandos*) formed up every morning after roll call; they marched out singing to the sounds of the camp orchestra in rows of fives. Passage through the camp gate, where the column of prisoners was received by a flock of SS officers counting the crews as they left the camp, presented a danger point. The next uncertainty had to do with the distance to the work site and the type of work to be done. The length of the routes to work fluctuated between a mile and a half or so and a dozen or more miles (see map 2). The traversing of even the shorter routes required an effort out of proportion to a prisoner's capabilities; not everybody could manage the longer routes on their own. Depending on the degree of terror applied by the prisoner-functionaries who accompanied the prisoners, a work crew could diminish in numbers even before reaching the site where the workday was to elapse.

Work was performed at a site guarded by armed SS officers (*Posten*) and trained German shepherds; direct supervision was given over to the prisoner-functionaries. How the supervision was carried out by these three types of functionaries, and what kind of work had to be done, determined how well a crew lasted until the time came for the return to camp. The way back in the evening was incomparably more difficult than the way to work in the morning. Men and women of failing strength were additionally burdened with carrying the dead and the unconscious, and supporting those who had no strength to walk on their own. Along the way other work crews passed by in varying states after their day-long labor. The way back was often dangerous because it was necessary to pass through the camp gates singing and at a marching step, with an outer bearing such as would not attract punishment; people were often singled out at the moment of entry to the camp grounds.

The gate was that point in camp space which bound together with a common fear rank-and-file prisoners, prisoner-functionaries, and the paid personnel of the camp; here loomed the threat of heavy penalties for everything—including lack of supervision. Unsatisfactory entry through the gate could result in death, a beating, and other punishments used on the prisoners, but also in loss of position for the prisoner-functionaries, and in penalties for the guards and lower ranks of the SS. Yet regardless of what awaited them beyond, all prisoners felt a vast relief on entering—to pass through that gate was to come home.

The dimensions of concentration-camp space: the length of the road to work, the size of the subcamps, the barracks, and the bunks and "roosts," were radically transformed in the consciousness of the prisoners living in that space. Because of the prisoners' physical deterioration, the way to work felt like a march many dozens of miles long—the onerousness of that walk was intensified by shoes that were suited neither for such purposes nor for the prisoners' foot sizes. The subcamp seemed like a large city divided up by a main artery and side streets. Crossing a camp section from one end to the other was perceived as a distance crossed on foot in a rather large city—in the prisoner's mind that distance was increased by the swampiness of the terrain, which added to the effort of getting around. The one-story shack that constituted a residential dwelling seemed like a large apartment house, and the collective bunk possessed all the characteristics of a home where the family group arranged its life.

Space and Communication

The crisscrossing of the two criteria for dividing up prisoners and space—according to residential groups and place of residence and according to working groups and work location—created additional possibilities of communication. In the work crews prisoners from different barracks met each other. The field crews that went to work outside had chances to meet prisoners from other subcamps. Even the fleeting contacts of passing work crews permitted some kind of signal to be made or the transfer of information. Lengthier contacts, in situations where men and women were working in close proximity or where a work crew under the supervision of an SS officer was sent onto the grounds of another subcamp, made possible not only the exchange of information but also the transmittal of things. In this way the crisscrossing of two divisional systems extended living space by breaking through the boundaries of isolated city-states and creating a system of communication among them.

This communication system suffered from the distortions that always result from a chain of oral messages. A group of women prisoners convinced themselves of the extent of these distortions in this way: while working in a field crew (*Aussenkommando*) under exceptionally oppressive conditions, which were depleting the last remnants of the group's endurance, they decided to float an optimistic rumor among their ranks, concerning an airlift of food supplies which, unfortunately, had fallen outside the camp limits. On their return from work, now inside the camp, they were informed of a surprise raid that was to liberate the camp that night and advised to sleep with their shoes on. In this way their experiment confirmed how extensive the network of communication was that broke through purposefully conceived administrative divisions of space. But at the same time it showed how imperfect that spontaneous system was, distorted by the need for hope in a situation where hope had no basis.

CHAPTER FOUR
Breaking the Prisoners' Solidarity

> *Not the strong who wield the power,*
> *but those who refused to submit to force.*
>
> *A. P.*

THE OBJECTIVE of a concentration camp was the biological destruction of prisoners. The responsibility for accomplishing that objective was borne by the SS who represented Nazi terror in the camp and had every means at their disposal for carrying out their ends. A relatively small group of SS, united by their common task, terrorized hundreds of thousands of prisoners deprived of every possibility of defending themselves. As a rule the manner of death was decided by the camp personnel, who were classed according to their official rank and organized according to the scope of their assigned command.

A proven method of terror, and one that was exercised systematically, consisted in shattering the cohesiveness of a prisoner group and creating a permanently threatening environment— threatening to the prisoner community from within as well as from without. One way of intensifying the threat was to entrust the most brutal and unbalanced prisoners with authority over their fellow inmates.[1]

The number of prisoners who participated in the apparatus of terror was very small in proportion to the great masses of prisoners who were subjected to that terror. Auschwitz is an example of the type of camp (as opposed to the women's camp in Majdanek, for example) for which expansion of the apparatus of terror by means of a staff of felons had been anticipated even in its organizational stage. To these criminals, especially selected from other camps, were entrusted key functions inside the camp. The manner in which these functions were exercised assured the continuity of terror during the absence of the SS from the camp premises. From the outset Auschwitz, as a collection of prisoners, was organized as a "paradise for green and black badges" [see chapter seven, "Colored Triangles"]; this situation prevailed the longest in the women's camp at Auschwitz-Birkenau.

In this way the most demoralized criminal prisoners were endowed with executive power and the right to choose their staffs from those prisoners who would be capable of using force of the most brutal kind in the exercise of their authority.

From the start there was a strict separation (an extension of the SS's scope of command) between authorities exercising power on the camp premises and field authorities in charge of the work crews. The in-camp prisoner-administrators—the *Lagerältesten*, the *Blockältesten*, and their staffs of subordinates—were responsible for "order" inside the camp, and for enforcing all regulations by the use of any means—murder included. In everyday speech "order" meant the observance of a strictly regulated routine as well as immediate response to incessant, non-routine, additional orders, verification of the number of prisoners quartered in each barracks, distribution of food and clothing, the state of hygiene

1. I am concerned here with the symptoms of degeneration of authority among prisoner-functionaries; those situations in which the assuming of a leadership function and the occupying of a higher place in the camp system were the consequence of loyalty to fellow-prisoners and the desire to come to the aid of others will be discussed in a later chapter.

in the barracks, on the camp premises, and of the prisoners themselves.

In practice this meant terror, brutality, and arbitrary punishments administered to individuals at random, because given existing conditions "order" so interpreted was impossible to maintain. The state of a prisoner's organism, wasted by camp conditions, rendered him incapable of rapid responses. It was impossible to observe the most fundamental rules of hygiene, owing to the unhygienic conditions in the camp and the lack of basic sanitary facilities (including water). Moreover, unfamiliarity with the language in which orders were given prevented their understanding and execution.

"Order" in camp also included various abuses of authority on the part of prisoner-functionaries: appropriating food rations intended for prisoners, stealing their clothes, accepting prisoners' bribes in return for good treatment, arbitrary singling out of prisoners for punishment, seeking victims to torment to death, preparing separate meals for themselves from stolen food, providing themselves with (relatively) luxurious living conditions in quarters that were separated from the ordinary prisoners.

Along with any position of authority went certain prescribed privileges—in practice the extent of these privileges was endless. After all, in a concentration camp the word "order" served to designate the whole system of living conditions with their specific objective—this was an "order" according to which prisoners, one way or another, were supposed to die.

Personal relationships between prisoner-functionaries assigned to individual barracks and the ordinary prisoners "stuffed" into those barracks developed relatively seldom. Various factors account for this. The possession of limitless power divided those who exercised it from those who were subject to it. The congestion in the barracks was so great that a *Blockältester* would not know all of his charges; also, the frequent changes of residents in the barracks (fatalities, transfers, new transports) as well as the transfer of functionaries to other barracks produced a situation where direct contacts were exceptional.

Authority over the work crews as a whole was exercised by a prisoner—the *Lagerkapo*—and a large staff of subordinate *Kapos* with their own staffs of underlings responsible for the individual work crews. This group of functionaries was responsible for the organization of work and its results, the dividing up and formation of work crews, escorting the crews to the work site, supervising the performance of work, accompanying back to camp those who survived the day and seeing that those who did not survive (but were indispensable for the accuracy of the records) were also delivered back to camp.

In practice the forming of work crews often meant beating the prisoners and driving them like cattle into the crews whose prisoner-bosses were most noted for their cruelty and their bullying (and who worked under the cruellest SS officials).

To a certain extent the work day and how it passed depended on the type of work, but above all it depended on the degree of degeneracy and the changing moods of the group of prisoners who supervised the work. Regardless of the type of activity, it was mandatory to perform it without cease.

The prescribed requirements of the work considerably exceeded the physical capacities of the prisoners; these requirements constituted an element of the camp system, hastening a prisoner's death. The terror and physical violence which accompanied the performance of work was also an element of this system, as was the murdering of those prisoners who were not up to the work, or upon whom the overseers vented their sadism.

On the whole the privileges of the prisoner-functionaries whose task was to oversee the field crews (*Aussenkommandos*) were many. All functionaries were exempt from physical work, received extra food rations, had better living conditions and a somewhat better supply of clothing than the mass of prisoners. Additional advantages were afforded by the work site: the appropriating of prisoners' food rations, and the taking of bribes in return for not maltreating them. The personnel of the work crews laboring outside the camp was generally very fluid, and for that reason friendly relations seldom developed between workers and functionaries.

A different problem was posed by the crews working continuously in the same place and with the same people and by the crews working with a roof over their heads; different relationships, a different structure of subordination, and cooperation developed as a result of the relative stability of the personnel and the incomparably better working conditions.

The SS, as superiors of the prisoner-overseers, took part in the overall direction of these operations, and in addition regularly influenced life inside the camp and the work in the field, interrupting the rhythm of the ordinary routine with their commands and personally tormenting the prisoners. They operated at different times and in different ways—both as superiors of the in-camp functionaries and as superiors of the work crews. Acts of terrorism were also engaged in by numerous guards (*Posten*) even though their official job duties called for nothing more than the prevention of escapes from the camp.

In analyzing the group of prisoner-functionaries who worked with the SS and applied their terroristic methods, one has to consider the road which led them to that cooperation. What motives, what convictions, what traits of character led to the acceptance of crime, to the pursuit of a place in the hierarchy of power, and to personal participation in criminal activity? To ascribe a conscious choice of definite values to them as a group seems unjustified. It is worth asking, however, what their frames of reference in the realm of values were as externalized in their behavior. Here an analogy should be sought with the motivational patterns attributable to the SS personnel working in the camp of their own free will—in spite of the fundamental discrepancies stemming from their different situation.

The prisoners had been deprived of their freedom, either as confirmed felons or as recognized political offenders, and compelled to be in a concentration camp. It appears that long years of living in camp conditions, acceptance of the camp system as permanent, and an uncompromising pursuit of biological survival brought them to a thorough acceptance of the authority of brute force. The choice to participate as a functionary in the authority of force was made in the face of the alternatives: kill and stay alive or be killed. Such a choice was usually accompanied in the initial phase by various rationalizations reducing the feeling of guilt connected with the decision. The more brutal the crimes perpetrated against the prisoners and the greater the personal benefits and privileges resulting from these actions, the deeper the moral atrophy—and rationalizations became unnecessary. The psychological mechanism which Bettelheim[2] calls "the tendency to identify with the aggressor" then came into play. The feeling of security and self-worth increased, thanks to the experience of power and the latitude of authority. Authority created a secure channel for the growing need of aggression and was a means of acquiring the material goods that enabled one to survive. Giving way before the dreaded power of the SS brought one to the point where "conscience" could be identified with obedience to that power. Furthermore, the participation in an authority that aroused fear in others brought on fundamental changes of personality. Greater participation in the mechanism of killing was followed by a gradual shift in consciousness: the world of the camp was no longer divided into "us" (fellow-prisoners) and "them" (the killers); now it was "we—the powerful" and "they— the defenseless." The weaker and more defenseless a prisoner was, the greater was the feeling of distance between him or her and the degenerated prisoner-functionaries. The degenerated

2. Bruno Bettelheim, *The Informed Heart: The Human Condition in Modern Mass Society* (London: Thames & Hudson, 1961), cited after Maria Ossowska, *Socjologia moralności* (Warsaw, 1969), p. 88.

prisoner, having experienced his or her own often painful humiliations and terrors, advanced within the accepted power structure to a higher position in the hierarchy of authority. By their behavior such prisoner-functionaries strove to make their positions permanent or even to improve them. Prisoner-functionaries, shut off from the camp community, were tied to their superiors—the paid personnel of the camp—in a relationship of direct dependence and obedience. Despite their complete submission to the existing power structure and their choice of the Nazi value system, many of them did not banish all human responses; these they expressed by aiding the few prisoners who aroused those feelings in them.

Besides these relatively unequivocal moral choices, others also took place—and these were the most dramatic. Some prisoners did not withstand the physical and mental torture. Under the influence of fear they joined the structure of terror, aware that they were participating in criminal activity, transgressing acknowledged values. For increasing the chances of their own survival or the survival of their dear ones, fearing physical pain that exceeded their endurance, they paid a moral price whose dimensions they knew full well.

CHAPTER FIVE

Social Differentiation and the Odds for Survival

> *We understood then that our separation was to last and that we had to try to come to terms with time. In short, we went back to being prisoners; we were reduced to our past, and even if some in our midst felt tempted to live in the future, they quickly gave it up—at least as soon as they could—having felt the pain which the imagination inflicts on those who put their trust in it.*
>
> *A. Camus,* The Plague

THE TRANSPORTS that arrived at Auschwitz brought men and women representing nearly all the nations of Europe, diverse social levels and occupational milieus, diverse cultural, religious, and ideological traditions, diverse personal models and value systems. In the face of the camp system a general levelling occurred, as these differences ostensibly lost their meaning. Subsequently, however, as in every larger collectivity, new criteria for social differentiation, new systems of dependence, and new sets of inequalities inevitably came to the fore. Differences that constituted the vestiges of a prisoner's life prior to his consignment to the camp and differences that defined a prisoner's social position in the camp determined, to a certain degree, the odds for survival longer than the Nazi projections anticipated.

If one were to formulate in rational speech the collective expectations of the mass of prisoners, they would coincide with the assumptions of the Nazi plan for extermination. All the data observable in the camp pointed to the impossibility of surviving. The hope of individual rescue (release, escape)—which was still possible in the jails—had to die during the first few days in the camp. Yet at the same time a new hope was born in many prisoners—a hope that was irrational in those conditions—that those who could stand it longer had a chance of holding out to the end of Nazi rule, and therefore to the end of the camps. Such a hope lived and had to live in those prisoners who felt supported by their struggling compatriots—and especially in those prisoners who up to then had themselves participated in that struggle against the Nazi occupier.

Concentration camp prisoners constituted an isolated group of people, subject to the effects of the same violence, vegetating in the same conditions and under a constant threat, anticipating the same fate leading swiftly to a painful death, but desiring a return to their interrupted and very different biographies. And this is probably the extent of the homogeneity in the prisoners' community. Now begin the differences.

Unequal Chances on Arrival

In the structure of a normally functioning society, it is not only psychophysical traits but also a person's social traits which define his or her place in that society. The role in which a person is cast in society is decided by a whole set of socio-economic and demographic conditions as well as the specifics of his or her biography. To every one of these traits some social significance attaches. This can differ somewhat according to the society in which a given person lives. Generally speaking, a social role in European culture is clearly differentiated according to sex, age, health, level of education, level of income, and professional specialization. All these indicators, which before they were entered into a prisoner's record at Auschwitz had determined the place of that person in the structure of society, also affected to a certain extent the chances of survival in the camp. However, we are dealing with a situation where the meaning of previous distinguishing criteria fundamentally changed.[1]

For the elderly, invalids, and children, European tradition had established a pattern of certain privileges to compensate for their lack of independence and incapacity for larger endeavors. The custom of caring and providing some aid for the weaker constituted, in society's awareness, a value which required no justifications. Moreover, neglect in this area aroused vehement social condemnation.

This situation was immediately and radically transformed inside the social structure of the concentration camp. Here the universal moral guideline of caring for the weaker was replaced by the Nazi guideline for exterminating as quickly as possible elements of fractional biological value, who were dispensable in terms of a labor force. Any form of physical weakness reduced the chances of surviving the camp nearly to zero. In most cases it cancelled the chance to be admitted into the camp, and instead formed the basis of the decision for immediate, assembly-line-style death.

Sexual distinctions, which in European cultures had been tied up with the different social and biological roles of men and women, distinctions arising from the division of labor, differences of social customs, and the forms and marks of respect—all of these were totally eliminated in camp; traces of these distinctions were reflected solely in the extra possibilities for tormenting and humiliating the prisoners.

Transports to the camp from the various countries of Europe brought prisoners who were accustomed to different climates. The lack of protective clothing against the severe climate of Auschwitz was sometimes bearable for people accustomed to such conditions. Prisoners from countries in southern Europe

1. See Poland, Główna Komisja Badania Zbrodni Hitlerowskich w Polsce, *Biuletyny*, and concentration-camp literature (especially reminiscences).

(e.g., Greece) could not stand the cold, and their chances of surviving were minimal compared to prisoners whose previous environment had inured them to such climatic conditions.[2]

A prisoner's nationality and citizenship (which before the camp had been generally associated with cultural differences) became a differentiating criterion with far-reaching consequences for his or her chances of surviving. Replacing national distinctions, pseudo-scientific theories of race began to take drastic effect by ranking the different nationalities of prisoners, thus spelling out for them their turns to die. That ranking decidedly foredoomed their chances of survival. First place in this sequence of dying was assigned to prisoners of Jewish descent and Gypsies (regardless of official citizenship and nationality) and the proof was their mass murder through the use of assembly-line techniques.[3]

Slavs (especially Poles and Soviet citizens) were put in second place; the expressions of this were the various methods of murder used against them at different times and the (unrealized) program of general sterilization.[4]

2. See, for example, Stanisław Kłodziński, "Swoisty stan chorobowy po przeżyciu obozów hitlerowskich," *Przegląd Lekarski*, no. 1 (1972).

3. After the arrival of a transport of deportees (often several thousand) at the camp, "selection" of prisoners for the camp and victims for the gas chambers was made on the rail platform. The victims were told they were going to the showers. The gas chambers—there were four—had been installed with imitation showerheads; they could hold up to 2000 people. The victims were herded inside with the help of truncheons and dogs; then, once the doors were closed, pellets which emitted a poisonous gas (HCN) were poured in through a chute in the ceiling. After about fifteen or twenty minutes, the doors opened and the victims' gold teeth, hair, and jewelry were removed before transporting them to the ovens of the five crematories. When the crematory ovens could not keep up with the number of corpses, the bodies were burned in huge piles in open pits; sometimes they burned all day and all night. The ashes were thrown into nearby ponds or rivers, buried in pits, or used for making soap.—TRANS.

4. Reference here is to the murder methods used at different periods in the camp's history. For example, in 1940–41 prisoners who were incapable of working—the elderly, the chronically ill, those with abcessed feet and legs—were regularly subjected to "selections" for gassing. Only Poles were being sent to Auschwitz during this period. Between October 1941 and February 1942, 8,320 Soviet POWs were put to death by an unknown method. Their deaths were recorded in the camp records. Analysis of those records showed that 653 died within 5–10 minutes of each other; the cause of death was recorded as "heart attack," but the POWs were young and healthy. The suspicion is that they were

Third came the other nations of Europe, for whom (as the documents show) the program of extermination or exploitation had not been precisely established. Only prisoners of German nationality were excluded from this plan; for this and various other reasons the odds for their survival were considerably greater than those of other prisoners.

Imprisonment by the Gestapo for political crimes, for being of a particular nationality, or as a hostage, or in a "round-up" interrupted the life histories of people who had been performing definite functions and occupying definite positions within the structure of the social group to which they belonged. The attributes indicating those positions and functions radically changed their meaning in the context of the camp.

From the moment of arrival in camp all previous economic differences were totally levelled: a dispossessed pauper became the equal of a dispossessed rich man. Only certain traces of former economic conditions remained, but they could act either to the benefit or detriment of one's chances of surviving longer. A formerly wealthy person usually arrived in camp in better physical condition than a person torn from conditions of poverty. But on the whole being accustomed to a comfortable life increased one's helplessness, and therefore one's inability to adapt to exceptional living conditions and heavy physical labor. So in this respect the former differences resulted in greater chances for the person who had already known poverty and heavy labor. In principle, arrival in camp eliminated distinctions of social rank connected with level and type of education, career, and occupation. But the matter was considerably more complicated. In a very essential way previous social differentiation did affect not only one's chances of survival, but also one's chances of a place in the camp's organizational structure. Hitler's program treated the

---

killed with phenol injections. Throughout the camp's existence (1940-44), prisoners who were shot were called out *by name*.

There was a plan to sterilize all Slavic prisoners, which was never put into effect. Only some Slavic prisoners were used in Nazi pseudomedical experiments to test sterilization methods. [Author's private communication to the translator.]

mass of prisoners (as, indeed, whole nations conquered at the beginning of the war were treated) as a base of unskilled labor. With slave labor so conceived, a higher level of education worked against a prisoner in various ways. A lack of experience at manual labor meant that his labor was, on the whole, less productive. The existence of an intelligentsia in countries subjugated by the Third Reich posed a specific threat to German feelings of national superiority and to the possibility of manipulating people with a free hand; a prisoner more highly educated than the SS officer and the prisoner-functionary wielding power over him aroused in his masters a violent hatred. The intelligentsia (e.g., university professors, clergymen, doctors) were sent to extermination camps in great numbers, and persons who possessed the external characteristics that were usually ascribed to the intelligentsia (e.g., wearing glasses) were subjected to additional maltreatment and beatings from their semiliterate overseers.[5]

On the other hand, providing circumstances were favorable, education and skills that were valuable in camp conditions, such as the professions of medical doctor, engineer, or skilled workman, and a knowledge of foreign languages (especially German) afforded additional chances to save oneself.

To come from a peasant milieu made no difference in terms of the concentration-camp program to a prisoner's chances of survival; though being used to physical work could increase those chances. As various analyses reveal, prisoners from this social stratum had very poor physical endurance of hunger, very poor adaptability to camp conditions and to daily terror. Their chances of surviving turned out, in practice, to be considerably less than the chances of persons from the urban working class.

Persons from working-class environments, accustomed to physical labor, to various forms of social cooperation, and to the necessity of coping with difficult life situations, had, it ap-

5. J. Kret, "Przyczynek do historii zagłady inteligentów polskich w obozie oświęcimskim," *Przegląd Lekarski*, no. 1 (1969).

pears, greater endurance and greater adaptability than peasants or the intelligentsia.[6]

Formulations on the subject of how much a prisoner's chances for survival depended on his social and career affiliation have not been sufficiently documented; thorough studies are therefore needed connecting them with the general area of research into adaptability, which depends above all on various psychological traits and the structure of the personality, and also on the level of intelligence and education.

Separate treatment should be accorded those prisoners (from various social classes) who arrived in Auschwitz as persons from society's fringes: criminals, convicted vagrants, and sexual deviants. This category was most numerously filled by prisoners of German nationality and the majority of them had considerably greater than average chances of survival. By reason of their criminal past they were most suited for performing camp functions as deputies of the SS (this does not mean that all of them profited from these possibilities).

Some prisoners arrived in Auschwitz almost straight from a life in freedom; while others were brought there after a long prison sojourn that was often accompanied by an interrogation and everything that went with it.[7] Certainly a long period in jail would weaken a prisoner physically, and in addition the prisoner experienced a great physical shock: after living in a prison cell, deprived of movement and air, he was thrown, nearly naked, into an excess of fresh air, to which his now flaccid muscles were unaccustomed. On the other hand, his psychic shock was somewhat less than for the prisoner who arrived in Auschwitz straight from a normal life. While in jail a prisoner had already come to believe the worst. And at first, for some, the camp seemed to offer a

6. There is a divergence of opinions on this subject; in the view of many researchers a higher level of intelligence and education increases the degree of endurance in extreme situations.

7. This refers to the methods of torture on which the Nazis relied in their interrogations.—TRANS.

better chance than being tortured or shot by Gestapo jailors. Then, too, prisoners who arrived with a group of fellow-inmates from the same prison were known to each other from their prison experiences. Prisoners from the same transport and the same prison, who had shared common experiences, mutually supported one another. A prisoner who had once said goodbye to companions who were transported to Auschwitz ahead of him could now expect help from them as far as their limited opportunities allowed.

Another determinant in the process of adaptation was the difference between prisoners who were sent to Auschwitz for resisting the Nazi occupant and those who found themselves there "accidentally" (e.g., through round-ups, hostage-taking, and the like). The former reacted differently to the camp, realizing that they were reaping the consequences of a conscious activity. Those who were there by chance found it more difficult to accept their lot; most of them were psychically unprepared for the terror of the camp. Often they were sent to the camp straight from the street, after one or two days in prison. In such situations the impact of the shock was so great that it inhibited the capacity to adapt, and thus the chances of survival.

Still another factor deciding a prisoner's chances of surviving was the time of arrival in camp, and that time was measured in two ways. The lifetime of an "old number" [see chapter seven, p. 92] counted both as length of endurance in conditions that were unfit for life, and as experience of certain forms of terror to which only some of the prisoners brought to the camp in its later period were subjected. Time could be an enemy or an ally; this was decided by the season in which a prisoner was brought to Auschwitz. An autumn or winter transport afforded little chance of saving oneself; a transport in spring gave one a chance to survive the worst of the *Zugang* period in more sheltered circumstances. Summer afforded time to adapt under somewhat less rigorous conditions—to adapt to the camp, enter into the rhythm of daily life, and make contacts with other prisoners. A prisoner who arrived in spring or summer had greater chances to safeguard himself for the winter than a prisoner in an autumn or winter transport.

These differentiations, defined in terms of biological, social, and occupational characteristics, do not yet exhaust all the basic differences that set people apart before they became prisoners in Auschwitz. To explain them one must pass from a sociological analysis to a psychological analysis of attitudes and personalities and into the whole complex realm of mental phenomena.[8] Knowing the objective circumstances does not enable one to understand why, among people with similar life histories, some were unable to adapt, meekly accepting their fate, and some were dynamic, capable of creating mechanisms of self-defense, egotistically fighting for their lives—fighting without hurting others and fighting as hard for others as they fought for themselves. Some people were capable of hope and of giving at least the appearances of optimism in hopeless situations, and some lost hope completely as soon as they entered the camp. Many questions can be answered by defining the place in which a prisoner found himself or herself within the camp hierarchy of terror. Yet it still seems that such an analysis falls short of completely clarifying these problems.

The prisoners in Auschwitz, except for the group of hardened criminals, arrived at the camp as persons who had been brought up within the system of European culture. Because they accepted the same basic hierarchy of values, and despite national, social, religious, and ideological differences, they were like one another in the most important respect: they took a similar view of Nazi crimes and a similar view of the perpetrators of those crimes.

Unequal Chances of Defense

The entry of a prisoner's name in the camp records was a "privilege"—compared to the situation of the millions who were

8. V.E. Frankl's analysis does not seem convincing; see V.E. Frankl, "Psycholog w obozie koncentracyjnym," in *Apel skazanych* (Warsaw, 1962). [Viktor Frankl's account of his concentration camp experiences can be found in *Man's Search for Meaning*, rev. ed. (Boston: Beacon Press, 1962).—TRANS.]

transported to Auschwitz, denied access to such privilege, and exterminated by assembly-line techniques. In practice this mark of distinction meant that the prisoner, designated with a serial number, had lost his former social identity and had been brought down to the lawless level of the camp.

In the community so designated, some of the prisoners wore an additional symbol to indicate they deserved "special treatment," which meant that their death was to be implemented with greater speed by intensifying the daily terror against them; or, if this did not produce the effect quickly enough (due to the organism's extraordinary resistance), that other death-dealing methods should be applied.

Initiation into the concentration camp was a severe shock for every newcomer. All of it was a shock: not just the sight of the camp, but the brutal welcoming of the *"Zugänge,"* the putting on of camp attire. Tattooing of serial numbers was also part of the welcoming ritual, but a later one; it was not used in the period when Auschwitz was being set up. The appearance and unhygienic condition of the clothes (often bearing traces of blood and feces), the shaven heads of women, the slyest and grossest words of abuse,[9] the pranks of the bathhouse staff (turning on alternate streams of hot and cold water), the beating, the shoving, but most of all the sight of the prisoners, not only those who stood for the apparatus of terror, but also those who were subject to it, produced shock.

A new transport of prisoners taken to the quarantine barracks[10] was immediately merged into the everyday rhythm of camp activ-

9. Z. Jagoda, S. Kłodziński, and J. Masłowski, "Osobliwości słownictwa w oświęcimskim szpitalu obozowym," *Przegląd Lekarski*, no. 1 (1972).

10. There was a quarantine period lasting about one month, and the quarantine barracks were isolated supposedly for reasons of disease control. This, of course, was absurd, since it was the internal living conditions and the diet that produced the epidemics of infectious diseases in the camp. The quarantine barracks were even more overcrowded than other barracks and acted more as an unloading point from which new prisoners were assigned to those barracks and those work crews in which the most deaths occurred. [Author's private communication to the translator.]

ity, into living conditions that exceeded one's wildest imaginings (hunger, cold, overcrowding, physical terror, direct, close contact with the most depraved criminals and sexual offenders). This first encounter with a whole set of phenomena without analogy to any previous human experience generally paralyzed one's self-defense mechanisms.

The first indications that the odds for survival were unequal among the prisoners showed up in their first reactions to the camp: there could be a complete breakdown; there could also be strained efforts at humor—symptoms of a vitality and a greater capacity to adapt.[11] We could laugh at our own appearance and the fact of still being alive; we could caricature the agents of camp authority. Untypical behavior could expose one to a brutal beating, but it could also take by surprise and bring, in response, only harmless invective.

The inequality of chances was also affected by whether, on arrival in camp, one happened to be met by people who offered help of some kind. The first forms of external aid came from the old prisoners who tried, to the extent they were able, to reach a new transport as quickly as possible in order to transmit the most important things to know about what was happening in the camp and how to save one's life. Even then not all new arrivals could believe this information, and not heeding it they forfeited their chances of survival.

Given the minimal possibilities of helping others, every gesture of goodwill, any form of material aid, even the slightest, possessed the greatest value. Whoever exposed himself or herself by offering this aid could not give it to everyone, and the choice was therefore determined by ties of blood, friendships with specific people, prison acquaintanceships, persons from one's hometown or region, persons of the same nationality. A great many of those who offered to help had had to go through their own first stage in the

11. See A. Teutsch, "Reakcje psychiczne w czasie działania psychofizycznego stressu u 100 byłych więźniów w obozie koncentracyjnym Oświęcim-Brzezinka," *Przegląd Lekarski*, no. 1 (1964).

camp alone and on their own efforts, since they had no support from anyone who had come before them.

The inequality of chances resulted from whether or not the person arriving in camp had the opportunity to meet someone helpful and what kind of help could be offered. Different attitudes among the new arrivals were distinguishable relatively soon, even in the *Zugangsbaracke*, by the capacity shown for cooperation. Prisoners from the same transport formed spontaneous "small groups," fighting together for their lives; but there were also persons who remained relatively alone, incapable of giving or seeking support. They yielded passively to an attitude of hopelessness and so lost their chances of survival. Some (very few) were also distinguishable by striving to increase their chances individually at the cost of the other prisoners.

In this first stage, when most of the prisoners still had relative reserves of strength, the small group created chances for those who belonged to it: the more resourceful of the group might acquire a better sleeping place (on the wooden planks, not on the bricks), they might "organize" a straw mattress, some straw or a blanket to protect them all from the cold; they might manage to get an additional bowl of soup.

The end of quarantine generally went together with the dispersal of these "small groups." The mass of prisoners, divided up into barracks and into work crews, had to seek support in new companions and once more get blanket, straw, and a place to sleep.

The first work assignments were, as a rule, the hardest. Sometimes whether one hit on the worst or the best work crew was a matter of quick reflexes and luck. Often this accident was decisive for survival. The possibility of changing from one crew to another depended on quick reflexes; good vision and quick reflexes could reduce the frequency of beatings dealt by the camp functionaries. The forming of "small groups" in these new conditions decided whether the quick reflexes of one prisoner would help him or her alone, or would benefit several prisoners who were relying on each other for protection from immediate danger, and also whether timely warnings could be passed on to larger groups.

One of the first and indispensable stages of adaptation to the camp was the cutting out of every superfluous effort—skillful simulation of work and the saving of one's strength for those days and hours when the terrorist overseers forced one to labor beyond one's capacity under the threat of beating and killing. If, thanks to the cooperative effort within small groups, the weakest member was protected, that—in the broad categories of values—was mutual defense. The weak member gained a chance of biological survival and had that important feeling of support. The stronger members were defending, in these most difficult of circumstances, their own moral position.

The possibility of surviving was reduced to a minimum by inability to work together and to work in self-defense against biological annihilation through hard labor. Those who did not believe the experiences of their companions, and thought their hard work would be appreciated by the agents of authority, lost their last reserves of strength and dropped to the bottom of the camp community. The deliberately slow pace of work was sharply exposed when a prisoner put his or her whole effort into the work. Anyone who distinguished himself from the anonymous group in such a way gained a one-time only chance for some extra soup; at the same time such a prisoner isolated himself from the group, fractured its unity, and laid open the weakest member—unable to keep up with the faster tempo—to painful punishments. He played the part of a strikebreaker, and if he did not begin to listen to his fellow-inmates such a prisoner was condemned to solitude. More so than the others such a prisoner rapidly lost strength and rapidly ended his existence.

The next stage of adaptation was a capacity for individual risk-taking—within reason. Depending on the type of work site, that might mean "organizing" some food or a place to hide away from work, or attempting to make contact with another work crew toiling near the spots where edible vegetation grew, and so on. With concentration and quick reflexes, such risk-taking made it possible to save one's strength or obtain extra food, but the least inattention could bring on every one of the camp punishments, loss of life included.

For most prisoners who survived the first period, this state of affairs lasted throughout their entire sojourn in the camp, although in general after the period of elementary adaptation new social mechanisms began to function, creating additional chances for survival (as long as this period did not end in the prisoner's death from exhaustion, beatings, or murder). For a few prisoners the action of camp mechanisms also opened up a chance to do lighter work in work crews with relatively stable personnel, and this afforded many additional privileges.

Short or prolonged stays in the camp hospital [*Revier*] were the rule for most prisoners. This "ambiguous privilege" provided an opportunity to rest, or to die in slightly better circumstances, but it could also mean sudden and unexpected death.

Some prisoners, as a result of taking a risk or failing to respond quickly enough, or because they were designated for "special treatment," found themselves in the penal crew [*Strafkommando*] isolated from their fellow-inmates, living and working in even worse conditions than the rest of the prisoners, and subjected to more intense forms of terror.

National groups capable of working together and groups part of whose members knew German had some chance, by exploiting the weaknesses of the German criminals in positions of power, to contain the brutality of the latter's actions, at least sometimes. National groups lacking these skills were condemned irreversibly to speedy extinction.

A longer period of time spent in the same *Aussenkommando* enabled a prisoner to anticipate opportunities and dangers and to profit from this awareness. If, for example, one of the SS guards [*Posten*] had a weakness for alcohol, then depending on whether alcohol brought on aggressiveness or an inclination for sexual intercourse with German female prisoners (with prostitutes mainly) or drowsiness, it presented either an acute danger or a chance to rest.

If the "bosses" of the women's crews possessed strong sexual drives and "organized" their satisfaction during work hours, it not only gave prisoners a chance to rest, but the effect generally was to lessen the brutality directed toward prisoners. In fact, it was the prostitutes, exercising their profession in camp, who sometimes displayed some human qualities: a need for childlike play, even the signs of sympathy.

The situations described above, which defined a prisoner's place and the limits of his self-defense, typify the conditions created by the camp administrators, permanently represented by formalized cores of terror. Because persons of varying moral levels, personality traits, and modes of social conduct had been cast into one melting pot, the longer the machinery of terror acted upon them, producing physical collapse and mental disturbances, the more intense became the conflicts (which existed from the outset) between prisoners. Besides the extraordinary (in these conditions) manifestations of solidarity, loyalty, and aid, there were also irrational and bitter antagonisms, as well as sharp conflicts of interest, thefts, and brutal fights.

The irrational conflicts developed along the dividing lines of nationality. The impossibility of communicating, due to the language barrier, led to the stereotyping of other nations (in a mold of largely negative and ridiculous traits) and to brutal actions motivated by irrational hatreds. The relatively small group of prisoners (mainly intelligentsia) who knew foreign languages could only slightly ease these antagonisms by acting as go-betweens in communication.

The diversity of social backgrounds possessed another significance. Initially the physical appearance and a few unconscious habits of the intelligentsia (often comic in camp conditions) evoked the scorn of persons from other backgrounds, while the realization that all were on the same level despite their different life histories sometimes gave rise to a specific type of humor, sometimes to satisfaction. Similarly the physical appearance and some of the habits of those who came from a peasant background aroused the mockery and contempt of those who felt they were better.

Class antagonisms, however, did not stand out as sharply as the national antagonisms, which consisted mainly of ridicule and manifestations of contempt directed at "foreigners." In a situation requiring cooperative effort, these class differences not only vanished entirely but were transformed into very firm ties of sympathy and solidarity. On the other hand national conflicts on a large scale were kept up and grew more intense wherever authentic conflicts of interest arose in connection with the winning of dominance in the camp power structure by one nation (besides the Germans).

Besides these conflicts and antagonisms (which were divisive and caused the mass of prisoners added anguish) sharp and violent conflicts of interest burst forth during the distribution of food and clothing and the assignment of sleeping berths. The more starvation advanced, the faster the incidents of stealing food—normally committed by the weakest and most helpless of the prisoners—multiplied. Crowds of filchers sprang up, hurling themselves at the food as it was being carted to the barracks.

Besides the organized terror, another, more elemental terror came into being: of the stronger over the weaker. This was the inevitable consequence of the whole camp situation. That someone participated in the violence or became a victim of the violence, or that someone happened not to take part in events in either role—these facts should not be evaluated in light of the normal hierarchy of values without taking into account psychological analysis of the disease of starvation and the mental consequences of prolonged exposure to the action of a criminal apparatus of terror manifested in every possible way.

Regardless of moral judgments, the fact is that the mechanisms of terror created a situation where some prisoners—by their very existence—restricted the chances of others to survive. And no matter what effect the situations we have just considered had on the increase or decrease of a prisoner's chances for survival, whether he survived or perished was purely a matter of luck.

CHAPTER SIX

A Place in the Structure of Terror

> *I was walking at night, fifth in the row. The bronze flame of*
> *people being incinerated flickered across a violet sky. . . .*
> *Anyway, that night, I watched a half-naked, sweat-drenched*
> *man jump out of a stifling cattle-car onto the camp's gravel*
> *platform, take in a deep gulp of the brisk, cold dusk, stagger*
> *over to another man and, convulsively gripping his shoulders,*
> *begin frantically to persuade him of something. . . . For*
> *many days afterward, I saw men crying over their pickaxes,*
> *their shovels, and by the wagon. I watched how they lifted the*
> *rails for the fence, carefully evened out the ground, stroked*
> *the sides of ditches with their spades, raised up barracks,*
> *watch-towers, and crematoria. I watched them waste away*
> *from scabies, inflammation, typhoid, and hunger. I watched*
> *others, collecting diamonds, watches and gold, providently*
> *bury them in the ground. Still others, out of snobbery, tried to*
> *kill as many people and possess as many women as they could.*
> T. Borowski, World of Stone

EVERYDAY LIFE for each prisoner meant long hours
of standing for roll call from dawn until the formation of
work crews and the march out of camp; it meant work
that exceeded the strength of the strongest, performed under the
permanent threat of terror, and the crews' return after work to
several hours of evening roll call. Afterwards, as a rule, the period
scheduled for rest began in circumstances which did not at all
conduce toward that end. Such was the routine regardless of the
season of the year or the changes in weather—it was interrupted
only by other forms of terror which disturbed this rhythm of
activities.

In this way some of the prisoners survived their whole camp
sojourn. The majority, however, at least for a while, encountered
either worse or somewhat better circumstances.

Penal Crews

Every infringement of camp regulations, such as making contact with a prisoner from another subcamp, carrying a letter, carrying food, snatching something edible from the fields, or possessing superfluous articles (e.g., a sweater, a towel), not part of a prisoner's regulation attire, brought down very heavy penalties. Among these transfer to the penal crew[1] was relatively frequent.

Prisoners in these crews were identified by a round, red patch on their backs recognizable everywhere; they lived under considerably severer conditions. Their food rations were curtailed; they were assigned to do the heaviest jobs under increased terror, danger, and beatings. They were prohibited from circulating about the camp premises. The whole set of conditions resulted in even more brutal exploitation of the labor of penal crews than of the other prisoners and the additional restrictions on them made it impossible to seek help for themselves. By regulation, prisoners in the S.K. [*Strafkompanie*] were isolated from the others. Some were sent to the penal crew for relatively short periods, after which they returned to the community of normal prisoners. If penalized for long or undetermined periods, a prisoner could only keep himself alive through immense physical and mental stamina and with the help of other prisoners who took advantage of any reduced vigilance on the part of the overseers to transmit extra food or medicine.

The Privileges of Relative Stability

Some of those prisoners who lived to return from the concentration camp owe it to the chance to work, for at least part of the time, in stable work crews. The odds for survival were greatest in

1. See, for example, Henryk Kuszaj, "Kary stosowane przez SS względem więźniów obozu koncentracyjnego Oświęcim," *Zeszyty Oświęcimskie*, no. 1 (1958).

a job with a crew that worked "under a roof" or in the smaller work crews that resided outside the camp premises.

It was not simply that such work sheltered one from the cold and was generally much less tiring, or that the roll calls—because of a real need (or an effectively suggested one) for getting the work done fast—were normally less prolonged. Nor was it because there were many more opportunities to "organize" extra food or clothing. These things were of fundamental importance, but they did not exhaust the list of privileges.

The way the work was organized and the circumstances accompanying it exploded, as a rule, the programmed concept of prisoner anonymity, breaking down the usual barriers not only between the prisoner and the lowest level of authority in the camp—the prisoner-functionaries—but also between the prisoner and the SS officials responsible for the accomplishment of the work. Crews that had relatively stable personnel such as electricians, carpenters, office workers, *Effektenkammer*, package room, kitchen and potato storehouse, even sewage disposal crews, and landscaping crews of the type housed at Rajsko,[2] and many others had the opportunity to get to know one another well and were usually supervised by the same officials.

With daily contact the prisoners' faces soon ceased to be alien. These prisoners who were living in better conditions (i.e., better than those who were tormented daily and anonymously in the field crews) began to resemble normal people; their looks no longer aroused physical disgust in camp officials. The majority

2. Rajsko (Raisko) was the site of a subcamp of Auschwitz, about 4 km. (approx. 2½ miles) from the main camp. The local inhabitants were evacuated and the vacant homes and villas taken over by the SS. This was the site of a laboratory, or Institute of Hygiene as it was called, which operated under the sole auspices and direction of the highest SS authorities. The institute probably served as a soft job for those SS who wished to escape the danger of the battle-front, but it served a similar purpose for those prisoners fortunate enough to have the skills and be chosen to work in the Rajsko crews. Vast numbers of specialized experiments in bacteriology, chemistry, histology, parasitology, etc. were carried out by SS scientists with the help of prisoner-scientists. (See the chapter on "Medical Experiments"—"Expériences médicales"—in Leon Poliakov, *Auschwitz* [Paris: Julliard, 1964].—TRANS.)

of the SS who supervised permanent work crews used the services of prisoners in various ways; multiple levels of interests developed and sometimes even an attraction to the prisoner as a person who, in pre-camp days, had had some sort of life story and social standing.

The prisoners, who were usually more intelligent than their overseers, knew how to observe and make use of their supervisors' weaknesses like laziness, desire for advancement, greed, desire to insure their family's material well-being, desire for great riches, fear of other SS officers, desire for a professional approval of their performance from a superior.

Prisoners working within the framework of this type of crew were able to form loyal, aware groups, to acquire a certain power over their superiors, and to use it for the good of the crew as a whole, as well as for the good of those other prisoners whom they might be able to add to the crew and of prisoners they might be able to help somehow, either sporadically or systematically, by virtue of the functions they performed. They had the energy and the opportunities to break camp regulations—supplying extra food, warmer clothing, and even medicines; they also acted as go-betweens for prisoners who had difficulty getting around and for isolated subcamps (e.g., the women's camp a and b at Birkenau, the men's camps at Birkenau, the camp at Auschwitz, Rajsko, the Gypsy camp,[3] etc.). To be employed in such a crew did not mean that one was protected from the camp terror, but it did put a limit on the terror. Neither did it mean that the situation was stable; there was always the threat that one could be transferred to another crew. It did not mean that every prisoner in such a crew spent all his time thinking about his more wretched fellow-prisoners; but the opportunity to help was there and it was often used. Nor did it mean that every such crew acquired influence over its SS official; yet one could say that in the majority

3. The Gypsy camp was established as a separate subcamp in Birkenau for Gypsies and their families. About 21,000 Gypsies passed through this camp before the last of them were driven to the gas chambers in 1944 and the Gypsy camp liquidated by orders from the highest authorities in the Reich.—TRANS.

of cases this influence was eventually won. Working loyally together, groups of prisoners were able to "supervise" SS officers during the inevitable reprisals carried out against the mass of prisoners.

Although the crews discussed above, and the prisoners lucky enough to get into them, constituted no more than a minimal percentage of the whole body of prisoners, they undid the program of terror in a small way by overcoming the barriers between "persons" and "non-persons" and by developing their capacities for various forms of organized resistance.

It seems that there is an observable pattern in the organizational structure of Auschwitz: the smaller and the more stable a group, consisting of prisoner-workers, prisoner-functionaries, and SS-supervisors, the greater the chances for blurring the boundaries between these three classifications and the greater the chances for forming humane relationships within the group.

Ambiguous Privileges

The right to be "cured" in the camp hospital was a prisoner's "privilege."[4]

Very few of those who were brought to the last stages of emaciation and disease by the terror and the living conditions in the camp and few of those beaten but not to death by the camp functionaries had the chance to be admitted to the camp hospital [*Revier*].

For those who were hopelessly ill (especially since there was nothing to cure them with) and for the severely wasted, it meant the possibility of dying a relatively peaceful death in a prone position and without being beaten.

For those who had some chance of surviving, it meant living in extremely bad conditions for a while, but without having to submit to all the regular and irregular commands, and without being abused for lacking the strength to keep up. It also meant that camp officials, terrified of catching some contagious disease,

4. See, for example, *Okupacja i medycyna* (Warsaw, 1971), a selection of articles taken from *Przegląd Lekarski—Auschwitz* for the years 1961-70.

would put in rather infrequent appearances for the sake of seeing order maintained. Although for some time the prisoner-functionaries in the hospital were quite often emotionally disturbed criminals, the acting staff of prisoner-doctors made consistent and effective efforts to change the functionaries and did their utmost under the circumstances to aid the sick.

With time a unique triumvirate took shape in the camp hospitals. On the one hand the hospitals, like every work crew, were subject to the terror of the camp officials; on the other hand political-prisoner doctors and the ever-growing auxiliary personnel, also made up of political prisoners, struggled with every available means to make sure that the sick were given some care and aid. Exercising their profession at the risk of their lives, they created in the conditions at Auschwitz supreme examples of the ethical practice of medicine. After some time, thanks to the organized work of prisoners, certain key points in the camp's framework of terror began to crack; the doctors were able to obtain by "illegal" means some medicine and nourishment for the prisoners—minimal, of course, in relation to the need—and they also received necessary information for saving the sick from other forms of terror.

At work in the camp hospitals at the same time were the German doctors, made famous during the war crimes trials, who infringed the basic rules of medical and human ethics, for whom the sick prisoner was a defective specimen of the labor force or experimental material.[5]

In the clash between these three centers of decision making (only in certain cases could prisoner-doctors make decisions contrary to official orders), the fate of a sick prisoner took shape. Hence the ambiguity of the privilege of being sick in the hospital.

The regularly repeated orders from camp officials to clean out the hospital by means of selection for the gas chamber created

5. See, among others, Władysław Fejkiel, "Eksperymenty dokonywane przez personel sanitarny SS w głównym obozie koncentracyjnym w Oświęcimiu," *Przegląd Lekarski*, no. 1 (1964) and "Etyczno-prawne granice eksperymentowania w medycynie a sprawa profesora Clauberga," *Zeszyty Oświęcimskie*, no. 2 (1958).

an objective situation where death, for a predetermined number of prisoners, was unavoidable. In the hospital barracks the camp's system of terror reigned in its most brutal form, and the ambiguous privilege of a respite from the daily terror was transformed into an immediate, quick death, most often by gas, less often by another means (e.g., by injections).

If information about an impending selection for the gas chamber reached the *Revier* ahead of time, the prisoner-doctors would discharge great numbers of sick people who could walk under their own power. Braving the curses of people wasted in the extreme, the prisoner-doctors in this way preserved the chance to save their lives.

Muselmänner—Beyond Chance and Judgment

As a result of hunger, cold, overwork, lack of rest, and the everyday as well as the extraordinary methods of abuse, the weaker prisoners—those of less endurance and those bereft of any sort of extra help—had to sink in a very short time to the bottom of the camp structure, from which there was no way back. Only extraordinary congruencies, an exceptional possibility to provide care and help, and an exceptional capacity for renewal on the part of the organism itself would prevent a speedy death.

Masses of Greek Jews died in this way, incapable of adapting to camp conditions, linguistically isolated, and left entirely to their own devices. Thus perished numerous representatives of all the nations herded into Auschwitz, who came from diverse social backgrounds, who were political prisoners, as well as prisoners-of-war, hostages, and criminals.

How this came about, how they perished, cannot be discussed in sociological or psychological terms. We have the right to consider the subject only in medical categories, and only in terms of our knowledge of the disease of starvation, its course, and its physical and psychological effects. Any other method would have to be biased by what we know of communities living in relatively normal conditions, by what psychologists know of the human personality from investigations carried out in very diverse environments, bearing not the slightest resemblance to the living conditions of a *Muselman* in Auschwitz.

A study of the effects of starvation in Auschwitz was made by Dr. Władysław Fejkiel[6] and he should be given leave to speak on this matter:

With respect to symptoms the process of starvation can be divided into two phases. The first is marked by symptoms of emaciation, muscular weakness, and progressive lessening of motor energy. In this phase the deeper damage to the organism is not yet visible. Besides more sluggish movement and overall weakening, the starving person betrayed no other symptoms. Apart from a certain excitation and a characteristic irritability, no further psychic changes were apparent.

It was difficult to establish the line between the first and second phase. With some, the transition was gradual; with others, fast. For orientation it can be established that the second phase began when the starved person had lost one-third of his normal body weight.[7]

Fejkiel describes several somatic symptoms characteristic of the disease: "In the initial phase of starvation people with a little character still managed to keep themselves in check, to preserve their human dignity, and their particular ethical standards, but in the next phase all ethical restraints broke down. The person behaved like a starved animal; he became totally unaccountable for his actions. To keep such people in some kind of social order, physical violence had to be used."[8] Fejkiel gives examples: a father stole food from his son, who was gravely ill; a stronger person

6. Władysław Fejkiel in his article "Głód w Oświęcimiu," in the anthology *Wspomnienia więźniów obozu oświęcimskiego* (published by the State Museum at Auschwitz in 1968) states that age determined the chances for survival (the years of greatest endurance being 18–30 years), as well as duration of stay in jail, individual constitution (short, small build), occupation, and social origins. Outdoor workers showed the greatest endurance (of weather conditions), peasants the least (traditions of bulky diet, difficulties of adjustment); white collar workers showed rather poor endurance. Youth and an individual's ability to adapt offered the greatest chances for survival. See also J. Kowalczykowa, "Choroba głodowa w obozie koncentracyjnym w Oświęcimiu," *Przegląd Lekarski*, no. 1 (1961).

7. Władysław Fejkiel, "Głód w Oświęcimiu," in *Wspomnienia więźniów obozu oświęcimskiego* (Państwowe Muzeum w Oświęcimiu, 1968), p. 12.

8. Fejkiel, "Głód," p. 15.

smothered his neighbor and took his food. Not morally aware of their actions, they stopped when their hands and feet were tied.

A starving person is indifferent to life. Those in the grip of starvation were incapable of resistance; they were transformed into passive dolts devoid of the capacity for cooperation. The few cases of suicides known to me from Auschwitz were committed by prisoners who were not really emaciated.

Nor is it an accident that in concentration camps an active attitude toward life and a desire to put up a fight was seen in people who somehow managed to get enough to eat. It was they who organized the resistance movement, the escapes, the sabotage, who made contact with the outside world, or who rendered aid to others.[9]

According to the calculations of the SS chiefs of staff, a prisoner could survive on the daily portion of food he received for about three months. After this time he was supposed to waste away and perish. The calculations of the SS were correct, although in my opinion applied only to young or younger middle-aged prisoners, who arrived in camp well-nourished and in good health. For others it was difficult to survive even the three months, especially in the winter and at hard labor.[10]

Medical science sheds some light on the conduct of those who sank to the bottom of the camp structure by evaluating it in terms of the symptoms of a disease brought on by the criminal activity carried on in the concentration camp. Along with this activity went various methods of abusing the dying. Some of the *Muselmänner* died in the hospital barracks and at least had a place to lie down, but generally they died everywhere: standing at roll call, being herded to work, in barracks and outside barracks, on the camp roads and in the camp toilets; they died unassisted or they were beaten to death. Of all the various kinds of death, the *Muselman*'s was one of the worst. From the point of view of the camp's structure and objectives, this sort of death was normal, and higher authorities used to rebuke or praise their subordinates for the statistical yield of their activity, encouraging them (with the promise of rewards) to increase their productivity.

9. Fejkiel, "Głód," p. 16.
10. Fejkiel, "Głód," p. 17.

The behavior of these dying prisoners often came under the criticism of stronger prisoners whose organisms had not deteriorated to that point and who did not realize that for the *Muselmänner* each successive phase in the process of dying was accompanied by psychic changes constituting the symptoms of disease.[11] A person who has never lived in a country terrorized by the Nazis is incapable of fully grasping the essence of that terror. A person who has never been a concentration-camp prisoner cannot conjure up all the mechanisms of camp life. The prisoner who had not sunk to the bottom of the camp structure did not understand the scale and variety of psychophysical disturbances caused by the process of dying.[12]

For the living this landscape of deaths constituted a permanent element of camp life. It codetermined their attitudes and either led to a complete breakdown or liberated the mechanisms of self-defense. The living could identify with the dying through compassion or through the vision of their own fate. They could also strive to detach themselves from the dying—ranging themselves with the world of the living, the others with the world of the dead. Sympathy could only be expressed in impotent rebellion. Only in exceptional cases could a sympathetic person help. By imagining their own fate prisoners lost the remains of their psychic strength, which they needed for self-defense. Prisoners who relegated the dying to the world of the dead could look the other way and pass them by or take their shoes and ration of bread.

Industrial Death

The organizational structure of terror in the camp cannot be fully understood without an analysis of the industrialized institution of mass murder. From the year 1942 a transport to the

11. Among others, Antoni Kępiński has given some attention to these problems in his works on Auschwitz. These works, previously published in *Przegląd Lekarski—Auschwitz* were included in a book by this author entitled *Rytm Życia* (Kraków, 1972).

12. "Wśród koszmarnej zbrodni. Rękopisy członków Sonderkommando," *Zeszyty Oświęcimskie*, Special Issue, no. 2 (1971). [A collection of manuscripts written by members of the *Sonderkommando.*—TRANS.]

camp meant that the prisoner who had been shipped there was condemned to inclusion in a collectivity destined for a sojourn in Auschwitz. In the beginning selection was done regardless of nationality and origin; subsequently it was applied negatively on a mass scale to people of Jewish origin. Selection was carried out by German doctors, who designated those capable of work— these were directed into the camp, and those considered incapable—these were delivered up to immediate death by methods which improved with the duration of the camp, while the output of the assembly line death industry rose even higher. During the period 1942–44 this industrial activity deprived several million human beings of life. This operation was carried out by the camp personnel in accord with directives from the highest government and party officials in Hitler's gang. The camp staff, besides implementing the mass murder, also showed its own initiative, perfecting the technology for killing as many people as quickly and as efficiently as possible. On top of this some of the SS who took part in the mass murders carried out their duties by thinking up individual little amusements which fulfilled a sadistic need.

Documents that have been preserved, especially documents of the *Sonderkommando*, made up of forced prisoner labor and mostly of Jewish origin, describe in detail not only the techniques of the gas chambers, the crematory ovens, and the obliteration of the traces of industrialized genocide, but also the behavior of the victims, among whom relatively few were aware of the immediate proximity of their deaths. There also exists detailed documentation on the way in which the victims' possessions were plundered; these goods were viewed as the property of the Third Reich and were sorted by prisoner work crews.[13]

The murder victims had to have been unaware of an impending death, because no normal person could have imagined other people, even the most depraved, to be capable of such deeds; thus gestures of fruitless resistance occurred very seldom.

The putting to death of people already informed of the scale

13. "Wśród koszmarnej zbrodni. . . . Sonderkommando," p. 170 (a description of the deaths of Jewish children).

and methods of Nazi crimes created situations of panic in the face of a dreaded death[14] and of additional monstrous mental suffering; it also evinced heroic attitudes that were expressed not only in a submission to the inevitable in the name of religious[15] and patriotic[16] values, or in the name of the most beautiful feelings of brotherly love for their murdered fellow victims, but also in an unequal and hopeless struggle.

The operation of industrial genocide was familiar to the inmates of the camp. Only the appearances of secrecy were maintained in front of the prisoners. As a rule the women prisoners in camps a and b at Auschwitz-Birkenau (separated from the men's camp by two bands of electrically-charged barbed wire, between which ran the railroad platform used for unloading the transports and the road leading to crematories II and III) and the men in the camps on the other side of the platform were witnesses to the process of selection for the gas chamber. The road leading to crematories IV and V separated two men's camps in Birkenau, and the prisoners in these camps could see it. All the prisoners in Auschwitz-Birkenau saw the crematory chimneys, and they knew what the smoke from those chimneys meant.

The number of people murdered could also be roughly estimated from the effects the victims had brought with them, which were sorted by prisoner crews. And despite the strict isolation of the *Sonderkommando* news from this source reached the inmates of the camp. News of where the transports came from and how numerous they were also came from the prisoners who were selected to enter the camp; and it came from the SS (especially those with small crews), who spoke about these things with some prisoners.

The threat of this assembly-line style death was a permanent

14. "Wśród koszmarnej zbrodni. . . . Sonderkommando," p. 112 (a description of the death of a transport of Hungarian Jews).

15. "Wśród koszmarnej zbrodni. . . . Sonderkommando," pp. 110-11 (a description of the deaths of a group of Poles, members of the Home Army, and a group of Dutch Jews).

16. "Wśród koszmarnej zbrodni. . . . Sonderkommando," pp. 53-54 (a description of the deaths of some American citizens from Warsaw and a description of the death of a Soviet POW).

accompaniment to life in the camp. There is no way of inferring how the prisoners reacted to it. Helpless despair must have gone together with individually devised mechanisms of mental self-defense. It appears that even those in whom all human feelings had been deadened by the camp could not last forever in an attitude of indifference.

If we try to manage an outline of only the reasoned responses, prisoners in their own minds felt themselves to be: (a) witnesses of very grave offenses committed by a terrorist mob of criminals, and witnesses also deprived of the possibility of counteractivity, and (b) directly endangered, because witnesses who could tell about these crimes would have to be eliminated together with the material evidence of criminal activity. Such reactions, which are readily intelligible to people who were never prisoners of the camp, were accompanied by others, more difficult to transmit: (a) for the time being, others are dying, but we are still alive, (b) some of the victims' belongings (food, clothing) will find their way into the camp and will prolong the life of some prisoners, and (c) some of the victims' property, useless in camp, but possessing great value in the categories of a free society, will end up in prisoners' hands and will serve to bribe the SS and their functionaries.

The Elite

The existence of hundreds of thousands of prisoners, living in the camp in conditions below an imaginable minimal survival level and dehumanized by a system of terror, constituted the social background out of which crystallized a strongly entrenched elite. Every terroristic system brings out such an elite; nevertheless it is hard to communicate the scale of the differences between the mass of prisoners and members of the camp elite.

It took shape through participation in the hierarchy of power. Thanks to their power, its representatives radically improved their own living conditions. To the camp elite belonged not only prisoners who knowingly and brutally joined sides with the apparatus of terror, but also those who acquired their positions thanks to a lucky accident; not only prisoners who implemented the terror, but also those who merely kept up the appearances necessary to preserve their privileged positions.

Membership in the elite—regardless of the functions performed (but depending on one's place in the hierarchy)—brought with it a special level and style of living which set this group apart from the general mass of prisoners. Accommodations for the camp notables consisted of separate quarters in the barracks, sometimes for a single person, but more often shared by two or three; they looked like ordinary rooms in a home furnished by their owners with great care according to their taste. They did not lack for a clothes closet with an elegant wardrobe, cosmetics, comfortable bedding, or a kitchen with a well-stocked larder.

An ordinary work day for the elite, who were released from all physical labor, was limited to the function of giving orders. The elite of various ranks attracted "courts" of deputies and helpers. A place in the hierarchy of authority enabled one to delegate any unpleasant or burdensome activities to other prisoners, who in exchange would be given a shelter from hard labor and enough to eat.

Depending on cultural level and tastes, each of the notables worked at making his or her dream of luxury come true. One might focus his energies mainly on gourmet cooking; another might concentrate on collecting clothes, changed several times a day and shown off on the camp's main street; a third might fill his or her room with decorative bric-a-brac. The level at which one lived was only one indicator of social position. Another was the size and composition of a notable's "court." A notable might employ not only a domestic staff (to cook, wash, clean), but also tailors or seamstresses, shoeshiners, hairdressers, and masseurs.

Such a court would still be unworthy of the name if the overabundant leisure time, which often brought on boredom and homesickness, were not taken into account. Social life among the elite required added attractions and thus arose a unique patronage of the arts. Famous singers, actors, dancers, and musicians were summoned to an organized party, and for a bowl of soup or a piece of bread enlivened the emptiness of these select receptions. Fortunetellers and circus people were also kept around by the elite, as well as erotic partners.

Among the members of the elite, not only social relations but also (perhaps especially) business relations took on a stable character. Friendly courts promised one another reciprocal services, supported each others' candidates for vacant functions, informed one another about any goods being traded, or acted as intermediaries in the giving of bribes.

The abyss between this select group and the mass of prisoners appeared unbridgeable. However, an SS officer's caprice had been known instantaneously to demote a member of the elite to the level of a common prisoner, whose fate, contingent upon luck and circumstances, could take various turns.

CHAPTER SEVEN

The Psychological Relativity
of Numbers

> *But what are 100 million deaths? Someone who has gone to*
> *war hardly knows what a dead man is, after a while. And since*
> *a dead man is intangible, unless one has seen him dead,*
> *100,000,000 corpses strewn across history can be no more*
> *than a foggy notion. . . . Ten thousand dead is equivalent to*
> *five times the capacity of a large movie house. So, to see things*
> *clearly, this is what should be done: get the audiences from*
> *five movie theaters to assemble at the entrances, take them to*
> *one of the city squares and kill them on the spot. At least one*
> *could then see familiar faces in that anonymous heap. . . .*
> *They made rough calculations, according to bulk measurement,*
> *with obvious chances of error.*
>
> A. Camus, The Plague

O NE PROOF that the SS in Auschwitz and their superiors were fully aware of the criminal nature of the
activities directed against concentration-camp prisoners
was the fact that the traces of the crimes committed were scrupulously obliterated and all records were destroyed and concealed.
In spite of this some of the witnesses of those crimes, and many
documents, have survived by various means—some thanks to the
camp's resistance movement.

It is known that millions of people were exterminated in Auschwitz; but the exact figures are not known. It is equally impossible
to reconstruct the national and social makeup of the imprisoned
or the number and origins of the transports whose members were
exterminated in assembly-line fashion. It is also unknown what
proportion of prisoners was sent to the camp by accident in relation to the numbers of political prisoners, criminals, or the

other categories of prisoners distinguished in camp nomenclature.[1] All these facts are important for an understanding of Auschwitz and the most careful investigation of these matters is necessary (at least on the basis of the fragmentary documents).

Size of the Apparatus of Violence

The average prisoner had no idea how many SS operated in Auschwitz. Regardless of their number, life in the camp focused on them, in the sense that the appearance of any one of them increased the danger of a situation, evoked dread, was signalled from barracks to barracks and from work crew to work crew; it inhibited all life-protective behavior that went counter to camp regulations. And it is not essential how small the group of degenerate prisoner-functionaries was in proportion to the mass of the imprisoned; what was significant for camp life was the fact that vulgar verbal abuse, terrorism, brutal beatings and lawlessness created an atmosphere of constant tension. The camp grounds reverberated incessantly with the voices of a few against a background of terrified silence.

In the anonymous crowd of prisoners, certain SS officials and certain prisoner-functionaries were well-known, and known not only by face. A prisoners' collective defense mechanism was in action, summarizing their knowledge of every authority who was a source of danger. It was known which of them would react the most brutally in specific situations. What to expect the moment a certain SS officer or prisoner-functionary showed up was also known. The traits of character, the habits, and the symptoms of good or bad moods were also known, for on these depended the prisoners' fates in particular situations. If a drunken SS man who was known for his cruelty appeared on the camp premises, his arrival touched off the prisoners' warning signals, and whoever was able took refuge in areas where direct encounter was less

1. See Anna Palarczykowa, "Władze hitlerowskiego obozu koncentracyjnego w Oświęcimiu, ich kancelaria i pozostała po nich spuścizna aktowa," *Archeion*, vol. 40 (1964); and Ludwik Rajewski, *Oświęcim w systemie RSHA* (Warsaw-Kraków, 1946), cited above, chapter 3, note 2.

likely; thus one man became a source of acute danger for all prisoners, and it was difficult to anticipate the direction his aggression would take.

The armed sentries [*Posten*] with trained German shepherds, who guarded the camp and escorted the work crews on their way to work, were not too numerous. Nor were all of them dangerous. The prisoners' warning system provided the information on which of them restricted himself to the performance of duty (prevention of escapes) and which of them directly endangered lives. The number of those armed with guns, truncheons, and trained dogs, who made up the dangerous apparatus of terror, was negligible when compared with the many thousands of unarmed prisoners. But the way they exercised their authority gave one the feeling that they were present everywhere; regardless of their numerical force they maintained full control thanks to their role in daily camp situations.

To a newly arrived prisoner and to the prisoner who had not mobilized his inner mechanisms of defense due to various circumstances, and had not joined into the system of collective resistance, all authorities were equally dangerous. To prisoners who were relatively adjusted, and who had joined the prisoners' resistance and information system, there were definite categories of the powerful.

Regardless of what individual traits distinguished the paid representatives of camp power, all of them to varying degrees participated in the crimes systematically perpetrated against the prisoners. Each person exterminated in Auschwitz is evidence of the guilt of the SS group who carried out the program of extermination. Statistically, for every SS officer at Auschwitz there were at least tens of thousands of people murdered.

Colored Triangles

One of a prisoner's basic identifying marks was the color of the triangular badge [*Winkiel*] sewn onto his or her jacket. A red triangle indicated a political prisoner; green was for a criminal, black for those sent to camp for vagrancy, and pink designated sexual offenders. Violet singled out a small group of Jehovah's Witnesses; they paid with a sojourn in the camp for belonging to a religious sect and choosing to follow its principles, which forbade participation in any activities directly or indirectly serving war. A yellow triangle added on to any of the colored ones, and so forming a 6-pointed star, identified prisoners of Jewish origin.

The exact number of prisoners who were marked with various colored triangles is unknown.[2] We do not know how many of them came and how many out of each category survived the camp. But figures notwithstanding, the identifying patches were often erroneous. Several things were responsible for this. A black triangle was just as easily given to those people who shirked the work that was obligatory for every citizen of the Third Reich and every inhabitant of the occupied countries. Besides this, one of the ways of disorienting prisoners was to use a green or black triangle to identify certain political prisoners whose attitudes indicated that they might become a focal point for organized resistance—with the result that the color of their badge undermined confidence in them among the "red triangles" (political prisoners), thus hindering cooperation with that milieu. A red triangle, in turn, was sometimes given to degenerate criminal offenders who, thrown into a community of political prisoners, could bring harm to that community. As a rule the red triangle was used to identify prisoners sent to the camp from prison after interrogation by the Gestapo, or without any interrogation. Very few were sent there as a result of any proven activity in conspiratorial organizations. The decided majority ended up in the camp without even the most casual sentence. The red triangle was also used for people apprehended in street round-ups or arrested as a result of mass reprisals, in which cases it was blind chance that decided who became a prisoner. In addition the red triangle was worn by people who had been arrested on the basis of the principle of collective guilt for an act committed by an unknown person; it was also worn by a very large body of children and

2. See Palarczykowa, "Władze w Oświęcimiu," and Rajewski, *Oświęcim w systemie RSHA*, cited above.

underage youth (according to the legal code of the time, a person came of age at the end of his twenty-first year).

Green triangles in the concentration camp also identified so-called "*SV*-ers" [*Sicherheitsverwahrung*], among whom were all prisoners tried by Nazi courts and found guilty of political crimes, in particular for the so-called "preparation of high treason." It was paradoxical that those Poles living in the territories annexed to the Reich, of whom it could not be shown that they had engaged in any specific activity injurious to the Reich and who had been captured in round-ups or as hostages, were given a red triangle in the camp, whereas often one who had been sentenced for political activity in the underground was given a green triangle, thus labelling him as one of the felons. At first this particular category of "greens" had a very difficult time of it: they were neither accepted by the political prisoners nor by the chronic offenders.

But it was not only the SS who counted on confusing the criteria of prisoner differentiation; many a time the mix-up coincided with a prisoner's own interest. A member of a conspiratorial organization, arrested in a situation which allowed him to simulate, produced, in the course of his interrogation by the Gestapo, evidence of his criminal activity. If convincing, he succeeded thus in cutting the threads which might have led to other members of the organization.

Hidden among Polish political prisoners quite often were Poles of Jewish origin, regardless of whether they had participated in the anti-Nazi conspiracy. In situations where the Gestapo was unable to establish someone's real name, this was quite frequently a successful ploy. There were sporadic instances, too, of a prisoner shipped in a Jewish transport managing to jump across to a Polish transport brought in at the same time, or of a prisoner in the camp managing (before the introduction of tattooing serial numbers on the arm) to exchange himself for a dead person with a different badge of identification. These situations required organized action—destruction or falsification of documents to which other prisoners had access.

Irrespective of the actual numerical proportions of the groups identified by different colors of triangular badges, the life of the camp can be divided into different periods according to the colors which happened to predominate.

Dominated by black, but even more so by green triangles, the camp was a place where the law of the jungle ruled supreme. Political prisoners were pushed out of every decent spot, driven away from the lighter work crews, driven away from water and from the camp toilets besieged by all prisoners. It also meant that a theft—of no matter how modest a camp fortune, like shoes or food rations—went unpunished. It meant a sizable curtailment of rest, being crowded out of a place to sleep, and the terror of the stronger over the weaker. During this period prisoners in other categories, out of all actual proportion, felt like a tiny handful compared to greens and blacks.

Domination of camp life by red triangles meant a constant and unflagging struggle to shelter prisoners from the terror within bounds of the existing possibilities, while trying to enlarge those possibilities. It meant a struggle to introduce and establish fundamental rules and standards of communal living in the relationships between prisoners, and punishments for those who broke those rules. This is, of course, a simplification. "Redness" did not always indicate "good," and "greenness" did not always mean "bad." But such a simplification certainly characterizes the main trends.

On the scale of Auschwitz's huge community, the Jehovah's Witnesses constituted but a tiny, inconspicuous little group; their number apparently never exceeded a few dozen persons. Nevertheless, the color of their triangular badge stood out so clearly in the camp that the small number does not reflect the actual strength of that group. This little group of prisoners was a solid ideological force and they won their battle against Nazism. The German group of this sect had been a tiny island of unflagging resistance existing in the bosom of a terrorized nation, and in that same undismayed spirit they functioned in the camp at

Auschwitz. They managed to win the respect of their fellow-prisoners (of various colors of triangle), of prisoner-functionaries, and even of the SS officers. Everyone knew that no Jehovah's Witness would perform a command contrary to his religious belief and convictions or any action directed against another person, even if that person was a murderer and an SS officer. On the other hand, he would perform every other job, even the most obnoxious, to the best of his ability, if it was morally neutral for him. The political prisoners struggled actively in the camp, organizing resistance and battling for the survival of their fellow inmates. The Jehovah's Witnesses waged passive resistance for their belief, which opposed all war and violence.

Letters and Numbers

Besides colored triangles, letters and numbers demarcated prisoners. Letters indicated nationality, except for the letter E which signified that the prisoner was in the camp for rehabilitative purposes. E was given to those who had been caught escaping from forced labor in the territory of the German Reich. What the percentage of the various nationalities of prisoners was, no one knows. In a prisoner's mind certain groups seemed numerous, others less numerous, but only to a degree did these perceptions coincide with reality. The impression of a given group's numerical strength depended, to a great extent, on the place it occupied in the camp structure.

Prisoners of German nationality seemed very numerous, because the decided majority of them belonged in the categories of green and black triangles, and they performed important camp functions. At the same time their aggression against other prisoners created the sense of massive numerical superiority. Among the political prisoners marked with the symbol of German nationality, Austrians were quite numerous; they cooperated with political prisoners of other nationalities, and during the period when the men's camp was dominated by the red triangles they played a large role in the tightly-knit resistance movement.

The very numerous transports from the prisons located on Polish territory suggest that Poles made up a large part of the camp community at Auschwitz. It is hard to judge how numerous Polish criminals were and to what degree they affected the framework of camp relationships. Polish political prisoners (regardless of what had been the real reason for their being sent to camp) constituted a group that began to organize even in the transports taking them to Auschwitz. They played a very important role in fighting the lawlessness imposed mostly by the German criminals, and in organizing unified resistance among prisoners of different nationalities. This group was very disparate. The red triangle favored the formation of attitudes of resistance not only among those who had, but also among those who had not participated in conspiratorial activity before being sent to the camp. The disparities naturally also produced essential differences in behavior.

The very numerous group of prisoners from the Soviet Union was also composed of disparate elements. Besides prisoners of war there were partisan fighters against Nazi occupation and a very numerous body of civilians sent to the camp as a result of collective reprisals. The loyalty of these groups, who at certain periods were maltreated more than other national groups in the camp, was very great. Territorial associations strongly affected the degree of unity; coming from the same region in the Soviet Union was the basis for the forming of many a small group. These prisoners were characterized by great physical endurance and liveliness. After the first period of isolation, prisoners from the Soviet Union and Poles began to form contacts and to co-operate, especially in concrete situations where cooperation was indispensable.

Although Yugoslav prisoners were relatively few in number as compared with Poles, Soviet citizens, and Germans, their presence was strongly felt in the women's camp at Auschwitz-Birkenau. A transport of Yugoslav partisan women arrived at the camp as a tightly-knit group of dynamic young women. They came into the camp like an army detachment, demanding the rights of prisoners of war. They alone forced the camp authorities to make a concession: they would not allow their hair to be shaved off, and they were the only female *Zugang* to stand out from the rest externally by their long hair. That exterior sign of separateness symbolized their great unity and determination to resist.

The SS herded representatives of almost every nation of Europe into the camp. Because some national groups were so few in number it would be hard to formulate even the most superficial of impressions. Rather, these would be accounts of single encounters. The prisoners who wore yellow triangles constitute another very complicated problem. This badge marked people of Jewish origin, regardless of their citizenship or national sentiments. Culturally many of these prisoners were incomparably closer to prisoners who came from the same country as themselves than they were to the mass of prisoners marked with the yellow triangle. This symbol was worn by people transported from Poland, Hungary, Slovakia, Greece, Austria, and Germany, and no criteria exist (but the Nazi) that would enable all of them to be treated as a homogeneous group.

In the camp the possibility of getting help of any kind from one's fellow-prisoners was determined by the possibility of communicating. Hence Polish Jews could seek help only among Poles; Austrians, among German-speaking prisoners. Greek Jews could not seek it anywhere.

It is hard to estimate the numbers of these groups doomed to extermination. For example, in the women's camp at Auschwitz-Birkenau it seemed to the other prisoners that there were great numbers of Slovakian Jewish women. Those who escaped with their lives from mass death won numerous camp functions.

Every prisoner remembers Auschwitz as being full of Greek Jews. They were a crowd with whom it was impossible to communicate, and whose reactions were incomprehensible to others. Incapable of cooperation and of organizing collective defense, they were the most tragic crowd—but often a dangerous one, because of its animated and absurd responses. They were a crowd that shrank at a terrifying pace, filling the whole camp with its dying.

That leaves the Gypsies, who were isolated in the Gypsy family subcamp, designated with a letter indicating nationality and with the black triangle—symbol of vagrancy, which after all constituted a basic element of the culture of this exotic nation. Their family life during their slavery, with flocks of hollow-cheeked children, and their collective death in the gas chambers, signalled yet one more phase in the history of Auschwitz.

Besides the colored triangles and letters—symbols denoting the categories of prisoners—there were individual marks, the tattooed numbers. Tattooing made it possible to identify prisoners to be deleted from the list without making the inevitable mistakes in situations where even German efficiency failed to keep pace with the statistics of death. Prisoners were tattooed with numbers on the left arm in the same sequence as they arrived at Auschwitz. The sequence of prisoners from the same transport was most often alphabetical. Jewish prisoners were tattooed with an additional symbol—a triangle—under their number.

These individual calling cards permitted prisoners from the same transport to recognize each other. A knowledge of the numbers made it possible to recognize prisoners from the same prison. Thanks to the numbers, ties between prisoners from the same region were maintained, based upon similar experiences and recollections from the prisons in Warsaw, Kraków, Lublin, Radom, and many others scattered throughout Poland.

High or low numbers were also significant. "Old numbers" (which meant the lowest numbers) distinguished the few who had come to the camp in its earliest phase, and yet had survived. These prisoners were bound by the ties of common experiences and sufferings from the camp's worst period of terror. The strength of this bond was such that all other distinctions—letters, the colors of triangles—paled before it.

Besides those who entered the list of prisoners at Auschwitz, millions crossed the camp's rail-platform who were never accorded the status of prisoners in the camp. In the subcamps situated along the rail-platform, the prisoners watched unending crowds of people herded on foot or transported by truck to the gas chambers. For many camp days and nights they breathed the smoke from the chimneys of the crematories. They sorted unending piles of clothing, shoes, children's toys.

CHAPTER EIGHT

Love and Erotica

> *. . . a feeling as individual as parting from a loved one, suddenly, from the first weeks, became the lot of a whole population and—together with fear—the principal suffering during that long period of exile. . . . But, and this is the most important thing, however painful was their distress, however heavy their nevertheless empty hearts, it can be said that these exiles were, in the early stages of the plague, the privileged ones. For at the very time when the rest of the population began to panic, their thoughts revolved entirely around the being for whom they longed. In the midst of universal affliction, the egoism of their love protected them, and if they thought of the plague at all, it was only in as far as it threatened to separate them forever. And so, into the very heart of the epidemic, they brought a salutary heedlessness, which one was tempted to see as cold blood. Their despair saved them from panic; their misfortune had its good side. For example, if disease took them, it happened almost always before they had time to take heed of it. Drawn from their long, inner dialogue with a shadow, they were plunged without transition into the deepest silence of the earth. There wasn't time for a thing.*
>
> A. Camus, The Plague

ALMOST EVERY concentration camp prisoner left his or her emotional life behind in freedom. Imprisonment meant a separation from the woman or man closest to him or her, from children or from parents; it interrupted marriages, or, in the case of very young people, it severed a first love.

The loved ones a prisoner left behind in freedom could, depending on the intensity of feelings, so absorb his inner life that the imagination, to a considerable degree, numbed him to physical pain, and as a result of the inner focus of his feelings, the fact that his life was in danger did not fully penetrate the prisoner's consciousness. The yearning and worry over the unknown fate of loved ones shifted the area of suffering into that which is the normal lot of those living in freedom. A mental situation was thus created in which the camp nightmare was transformed into a terrible dream-vision lived through in a state of semi-consciousness, while the prisoner's conscious mind centered on his emotional life.

If a prisoner had been snatched from a family structure in which he functioned as the main provider, and he feared that no one would carry on his function for him, this intensified the degree of his suffering, but it also strengthened his will to live. He felt necessary to his loved ones. He mobilized all his psychic resources, and only when overtaken by extreme physical exhaustion did he surrender to the inevitable. Every sign that his loved ones were managing without him reduced his suffering but also changed his motivation: he became a person who waited for help from them. Every sign of helplessness or danger to his loved ones turned the food-package that rescued his strength into a drama, since on his account his loved ones were going hungry.

If a prisoner had been wrenched from a structure in which he was the object of his loved ones' care and attention, sometimes the egocentric suffering was deepened: he developed a sense of the scale of his own unhappiness, measured by the distance from that situation in which he had functioned as the focal point for all tenderness, care, and rapture. Sometimes there was a basic personality change: from a person permitted to exist in a passive role by a former situation, he became dynamic, capable of active feelings, as the new situation liberated traits of a hitherto latent personality.

An active love enabled a prisoner to concentrate on his anxiety over those left behind; the knowledge that they had been spared a Nazi reprisal accompanied that love and provided a motive for quiet joy. The scale of such joy was a good deal higher for prisoners arrested by the Gestapo in place of their wives, husbands, parents or children. Every physical suffering and every form of torment was then taken as an act of love, with the full realization that the worst of all these things could have been done to the loved one.

The prisoners in camp sometimes learned of the loss of their dear ones, their betrayal or death. Betrayal broke a prisoner's frail psychic resources. This broken faith could be restored only through deep friendships in the camp. Or it could also be lost entirely, brutally trampled in the struggle for existence in camp. Despair over the death of a loved one could lead to a state of utter numbness and indifference to one's own fate. It could liberate a reckless courage, but it could equally well awake kindness for all who were suffering—a kindness born out of the deepest depths of suffering.

Still different was the love of those who ended up in the same concentration camp. Regardless of whether they could be together (e.g., mother and daughter) or whether they were separated by the subdivided camp space (e.g., husband and wife), their nearness in distance and their common sufferings could liberate dynamic, heroic attitudes. They developed a capacity for risk-taking in order to obtain food for the loved one and to seek help for that person. Camp reality was filled in by the concentrated effort to gain a glimpse of the loved one, if only from a distance, to gain information about the living circumstances of the loved one so that every possible help could be given that might increase his or her chances of survival, and also to conceal one's own suffering, which might cause the loved one to weaken in spirit.

At the same time, in situations of direct and immediate danger, the desire for life sometimes turned out to be stronger than the bond with a loved one. These were the most strenuous tests of human feelings; they were ultimate decisions—love or death.

Besides stabilized, familial love, the camp interrupted happy lovers just at the time of their most intense first feelings. The charm of a life about to flower was cut off and the feeling of loneliness made deeper. The emotional life of a prisoner in the midst of a first love was filled with yearning for the physical and emotional nearness of the beloved. This yearning isolated him from his environment, which he experienced—at least in the first phase—as if in a narcotic stupor. His new feelings—still untried by life's ordeals, conflicts, difficult living conditions—functioned within him like a living mythology of perfection. His imagination localized in this one person all the world's goodness and beauty, and in the face of the prisoner's own image of his self-worth, all camp criteria receded into the background. The secret of his love bestowed worth.

Regardless of external circumstances, of the course of life and death in the camp, the most important link with the world was the prisoner's bond of feelings. Only situations of extreme exhaustion and psychic disturbance resulting from starvation and disease could extinguish the sense of that bond; sometimes it endured to the very end.

Exceptional situations and fleeting encounters between prisoners from the women's and men's camps awakened emotional needs. In the conditions of camp terror only a few great loves developed. From the very outset they were stripped of the secrecy that unites lovers. They could only exist with the help of other prisoners who transmitted their words and letters and "organized" meetings. A great love in the camp created a legend; it was surrounded by loyal help and silence.[1] The secret of the two lovers was guarded from the SS authorities by all prisoners (even prisoner-functionaries). And sometimes an SS officer did not react with a denunciation when he intercepted a love-letter. For concentration-camp prisoners the phenomenon of a great love was like a sign from another world, a proof that even "in there" feelings uniting free people could occur. In the conditions of terror the common watch over this love created an optimistic bond among prisoners.

In the context of camp conditions the word eroticism evinces a negative reflex that has become entrenched thanks to concentration-camp literature. But after all the word has many connotations (not only in the camp) and such a confused sphere of

1. See, for example, Wiesław Kelar, "Edek i Mala," *Zeszyty Oświęcimskie*, no. 5 (1961).

human affairs cannot be written off in simplistic fashion. The difference of scenery imparts a different aesthetic value to such erotic liaisons in the minds of those on the outside.

For camp conditions other categories must be found, and only then can the various meanings of camp eroticism be established. In the camp erotic needs were not primary needs; someone who is starving, tormented and suffering from biological exhaustion feels none. It was a better physical condition, which depended on standing higher in the camp structure or having the privilege of receiving food packages, that defined the particular socio-economic category of people for whom erotic needs existed.

The spatial subdivision of the camp which segregated women and men meant that married couples and people strongly attached emotionally lived in close proximity yet in total isolation from each other. Only in exceptional circumstances could their bond of feeling find erotic fulfillment. Both parties ran a risk that can only be measured by the scale of their yearning. The discovery of such a situation exposed them both to humiliation and the heaviest of camp penalties.

Spatial segregation of the sexes also led to the spread of homo-sexuality among the healthier and better nourished prisoners in the camp. Authentic, emotional relationships of a homosexual nature developed and in camp conditions it was possible to actualize them. Through an erotic union loving couples consum-mated all their mutually protective feelings, expressed through mutual concern and often great risk-taking in defense of the beloved. Besides the sphere where eroticism constituted an ele-ment of mutual love, numerous situations arose that resembled ordinary marriages of convenience. In such marriages the emo-tionally committed partner often took care of the uncommitted partner. Sometimes a confirmed homosexual would lead a pris-oner of normal inclinations into homosexual practices. Such arrangements were usually deeply immoral or deeply demoraliz-ing. A prisoner-functionary's desire to satisfy his or her pederastic sexual needs could also manifest itself in various brutal forms of terror and blackmail used to bring the partner into compliance.

Besides couple-relationships, paid prostitution existed in the camp and the choice of erotic partners was dictated by one's ability to pay—either in the form of help in gaining a better place in the camp structure or, at each visit, in the form of food or better clothes. Homosexual erotic availability became a coin of incommensurate worth, in return for which the chance of biological survival could be won, depending on a client's possibilities.

A unique situation developed during the period when rather numerous male work crews would come to work in the women's camp. More or less permanent bisexual relationships started up among the women prisoner-functionaries (especially the *Blockältesten*), who had food supplies and separate quarters, and the men who were interested in the material aid (regardless of the allure of an erotic relationship). These liaisons played yet another role which was very important for improving relations within the women's camp. The group of prisoner-functionaries in the women's camp allowed their sexual partners to acquire a very large influence over them. The men used their influence to shelter the mass of women prisoners from the functionaries' aggression and also to see that camp functions were handed out to the prisoners.

For those who had loved ones close by, but separated by barbed wire, the chance to meet also increased thanks to the daily visits of the men's work crews to the women's camp. Because the personnel of these crews was stable as a rule, the loyal help of these male prisoners enabled married couples and lovers to meet, as well as parents and their children. These meetings fortified the prisoners' inner strengths and hardened their resistance to camp destiny.

CHAPTER NINE

Socio-Economic Defense Mechanisms

> *Nor will thought save the world, neither intellect, nor under-*
> *standing, but something quite opposite: that irrational hope,*
> *man's enduring desire to remain alive, his urge to keep*
> *breathing as long as possible, his small, stubborn, and*
> *laughable daily heroism in the face of misery.*
>
> *Ernest Sabato,* On Heroes and Tombs

THE TASK of a camp official was to exterminate the prisoner within an established length of time. The aim of the prisoner who did not passively submit to this fate was to prevent or hinder the officials from accomplishing this task. A prisoner's obligatory submission to all camp orders and prohibitions was tantamount to the accomplishment of the murder. Mental submission to the constantly threatening atmosphere hastened the process of this slow death. The average prisoner seldom had the chance to "philosophize"; he reckoned up his experiences, observations and reflections only in rare moments of relative quiet. Seldom was he capable of analyzing his situation, of reacting to that situation, and of considering the priorities of accepted values. Mostly he was forced to act spontaneously and instinctively in immediate reaction to actual events presenting a greater or lesser threat to his existence, which could affect his chances of survival. Nevertheless, spontaneous behavior among those prisoners whose physical deterioration had not yet brought about serious psychic disturbances did exhibit a more or less conscious hierarchy of values, the result of more or less conscious convictions. Prisoners' individual reactions, their reactions as members of small spontaneously formed (and frequently fragmented) groups, and their organized reactions were expressions of their outlook on life and their values, which changed under the influence of the relations and conditions in the camp.

Regardless of how isolated a prisoner felt or of how aware he was of the support of his fellow-prisoners, that support existed. In the beginning the chance to give material help was almost nonexistent, but there was at least human sympathy. With time, newer and better-organized mechanisms of collective defense made their appearance. The chances of their succeeding depended on the attitudes of large numbers of prisoners and their capacity for cooperation and loyalty in the face of the most acute terror.

Collective defense also depended on the influx of various goods to the camp market and on certain symptoms of demoralization among the camp officials and functionaries that could be used to the prisoner's advantage, such as the lack of solidarity, greed, bribe-taking and, in the criminal groups who lacked inner cohesion, specific enmities and accounts to settle between members and jealousy over the distribution of profits.

At Auschwitz the prisoners, or at least some of them, won greater real chances for survival from the moment when the "market" began to function and, together with it, the laws of the marketplace.

The Function and Evolution of the Camp Market

The first items to go into circulation on the camp market were prisoners' food rations—not only their regular portions, which they were willing to forego in order to get better shoes or cigarettes, but also food expropriated by prisoners who took part in its distribution (i.e., the kitchen crew, the *Blockältesten*, etc.); thus a prisoner who had a surplus of margarine, for example, might wish to exchange it for other food or for some other necessary article. Simultaneously, farm crops (raw potatoes, carrots, etc., depending on the season of the year) acquired by the crews working out in the fields came on the market.[1] Some prisoners were bold enough to eat their acquisition during work hours; some dared to bring it through the camp gates (risking severe penalties) in order to trade it for something else, or for a friend who lacked such possibilities. Goods also came on the market from prisoners working in the kitchens or in the SS barracks; other goods were brought in by the work crews used during the arrival of a transport, or by the crews that sorted clothes. Coupons for the canteen were also an article of barter, as were the very few commodities to be gotten there. One type of article could be used to buy a different type of article from another prisoner in the same situation. Sometimes (in favorable circumstances and with a desirable commodity), one could bribe the prisoner-functionaries on the barracks staff and remain for one day on the grounds of the camp, without going out with a work crew. In time the market's wealth was increased by the modest inheritances of the dead. A better sleeping spot left vacant by someone's death was also an article of trade.

Fundamental changes in the nature of the market took place above all in connection with the implementation of assembly-line techniques of killing and the introduction of the sometimes very costly belongings of the murdered victims (who had brought their most valuable possessions with them) and, finally, in connection with the permission to send food packages to the prisoners.

Prisoner crews, supervised by an SS officer and prisoner-functionaries, were utilized to transfer and sort the belongings of those sent to the gas chambers. It was their job to classify,

1. See, for example, "Wśród koszmarnej zbrodni. Rękopisy członków Sonderkommando," *Zeszyty Oświęcimskie*, Special Issue, no. 2 (1971), cited above, chapter 6, notes 12–16.

clean, and pack for shipping to Germany those articles considered to be the rightful property of the Third Reich. Among these articles were huge amounts of inviting-looking food and clothing, as well as money and jewelry. How much warm clothing and food would find its way into the camp and by what means depended on the prisoners' ingenuity and boldness.

In spite of the permission from the authorities to send food packages, only a certain number of prisoners had the opportunity to receive packages; moreover, the caloric value and desirability of the packages varied widely, depending on the senders' possibilities. Sometimes, thanks to diverse individual and collective strategies, names and numbers of prisoners not receiving packages managed to be passed on to the "outside," causing food packages to be sent to them. Packages that came for prisoners who had died in the camp were, as a rule, returned to the senders. Packages that came (for a while they came in great quantities) from the families of Jews who were murdered immediately after arrival in Auschwitz were fated for the kitchens of the SS. How many of those packages would reach the camp or hospital barracks and by what means depended on the ingenuity and daring of the prisoners working in the package depot.

Within the community of prisoners, recipients of packages became a privileged group; they had the extra food necessary for survival, they had the possibility of sharing it with their closest friends and they had the possibility of purchasing warmer clothes on the camp market. The contents of the packages also constituted an internal camp currency with which to buy lighter work assignments from the prisoner-authorities and limits on the daily persecution.

Packages played a huge role in the life of the camp. They delayed the biological deterioration of their possessors, and often (but not always) that of their friends. They also made a breach in the structure of terror exercised by prisoner-functionaries, who at the time came mainly from criminal milieus (especially in the women's camp) and who were deprived of similar privileges. A middle-level prisoner-functionary possessed a certain latitude of authority, but none of the extremely desirable economic commodities which the prisoner subject to his authority did possess. A period of "petty briberies" set in that was extremely important for the prisoners' self-defense. In exchange for butter, an onion, sugar, or a sausage, a prisoner might save himself or another person. He could buy a good mood from an "authority" who was more interested in tasty food than in keeping watch over the "order" in the barracks or at work. Dialogue on a business level opened up, which broke down the barrier imposed by one's place in the camp structure and created a loophole in obligatory behavior.

The property left behind by the murdered victims made an even greater breach in the camp structure. Warm sweaters, blankets, comfortable shoes, medicine and food made their way into the camp, both as a form of unselfish aid for a comrade and as a commodity on the market. Market prices for a commodity fluctuated sharply, depending on the supply. Periodic expansion of the food supply from outside the camp and its circulation through the market contributed to the radical fluctuations in price for such articles as camp food and camp clothing. Depending on supply one paid anywhere from five to ten cigarettes for a piece of camp bread, but sometimes one cigarette would do. As those prisoners who stood higher in the camp hierarchy and those who received good packages began to feed themselves mainly with food from outside the camp, thefts of ordinary prisoners' food rations declined. In some periods the number of prisoners interested in the camp soup declined, and this gave the rest a chance to receive additional portions. All the possibilities arising out of the changed market structure were not, of course, available to everyone. The majority starved and died regardless of camp trade. However, the black market saved the lives of many prisoners.

The role of this market was extremely important and it affected the structure of relations in the camp. The dimensions of the plundered property and its range of quality were so great that the situation produced another breach in the power structure, this time within the group of SS. Certain arrangements were worked out between the particular group of professional murderers and the prisoners through whose hands (by reason of their work) passed objects of great value. Many SS officials desired to appropriate some of these goods in a systematic way. Owing to the camp's hierarchical structure, they were seldom able to do it individually and "with their own hands." Knowing themselves and their SS colleagues, they collaborated with each other only in exceptional cases, when their mutual services—like a double-edged weapon of blackmail—guaranteed mutual loyalty.

Greed, therefore, compelled them to cross the uncrossable line and to enter into contact with prisoners. In the case of a one-time appropriation, a prisoner could be used as a tool and then exterminated as a witness. In the case of systematic thefts, he became an indispensable partner, who chose the most valuable goods for the SS officer and helped him toward his goal, which was to get rich. In this way some of the SS officials came to depend on prisoners, who could in turn skillfully make demands of their own. A currency strong enough to buy the services of SS officials and prisoner-functionaries had made its appearance inside the camp. New groups of interests arose, linking particular officials with prisoners who were no longer anonymous. Within the SS mob of murderers, a relatively innocent (compared to their regular assignment) activity started up, that went counter to administrative orders and had to be concealed from their superiors and from other members of their group. This activity considerably weakened the effectiveness of some SS officers. For many of them getting rich had become their main objective, and striving toward it consumed some of the energy which had formerly gone into winning a promotion in the official hierarchy. Some—those who previously had not seen their place in society outside of that hierarchy—experienced a new vision of power in the form of riches. To this "lyricism over money" among the SS many people owe their lives. Some are aware of it, others are not.

The Battle for Power

Auschwitz, as we mentioned before, began operation as a "paradise" for prisoners wearing black and green triangles. The first gang of them was especially selected and brought there from other camps (for example, the group of prisoners from Sachsenhausen [a Nazi camp in Germany] with life sentences for murder) to fill the main functions in Auschwitz. Red triangles—that is, political prisoners of various nationalities—were made totally subject to the authority of professional criminals. At that time only a few political prisoners who were of German nationality had the opportunity to win a higher place in the hierarchy of power.

As the first transports of prisoners began dying off and thousands of newcomers poured in, some of those who survived the worst period managed to acquire various, but for the time being only minor, camp functions. In addition, certain necessary jobs arose inside the camp, requiring special qualifications. A German prostitute could perform the function of *Blockälteste* or *Kapo* perfectly well, but she could not do office work or any other type of work requiring skill and intelligence. The obtaining of such a function afforded better chances of survival, thanks to the lighter work load and the extra food. It also gave one a certain range of possibilities of authority which, depending on the person who had won that function, could be made use of either for the saving of oneself alone (without thinking of others) or for the saving of oneself and others. It is hard to establish which of these motives was more frequent at the moment the prisoners undertook the functions. Conclusions can be drawn, however, from the way prisoners used those functions. As a rule every kernel of power in the hands of a person who retained even the minimum of human values increased the possibilities of resisting, and created the chance to decide (or at least propose) whom to entrust with another function or whom to assign to lighter work. The prisoner-functionary ceased to be anonymous; his or her strength of nerves, initiative, and shrewdness constituted the assets of a group of prisoners. If resourceful, the functionary established the kinds of contacts through whom his or her charges could be "pushed". For example, if the functionary worked in an office under the immediate supervision of an SS officer (e.g., *Schreibstube, Politische Abteilung*), he or she then had the opportunity to recommend fellow-prisoners for work. In this way groups of informally organized prisoners who trusted one another and worked together in confidence gradually took control of the centers of camp power.

Higher positions in the camp hierarchy grew more numerous as the population of the camp rose and the necessity to enlarge the number in command became apparent. The number in charge of sorting plundered property also had to increase as a result of the scores of transports sent to the gas chambers. At the same time positions were vacated by prisoner-functionaries who either died, were punished by removal from their posts, or were transferred to other camps.

Even though according to the Nazi program the intelligentsia and the members of the resistance movement were to be ruthlessly exterminated, thanks to their qualifications, to their mutual loyalty, and to their capacity for working together, the political prisoners managed a gradual seizure of power. This process took place in the men's camp at Auschwitz and at Auschwitz-Birkenau.

The rescue strategy of reserving the best places in the camp structure for one's intimates was applied universally. Characteristically intimacy (besides blood relationship or previous acquaintance) was defined by nationality. Linguistic and cultural barriers were so strongly experienced that, in the extremity of the concentration-camp situation, only a person of the same nationality could be counted on for the long run. In the women's camp at Auschwitz-Birkenau, this attitude was more firmly entrenched owing to the behavior of the "green triangles" (who held on to their power for a very long time). In such situations non-German prisoner-functionaries presented a real threat to other prisoners.

The degree of terror employed on all prisoners largely depended on what group controlled the middle levels of camp power—on what nationality it was (and what color of triangle predominated), what kind of values its members had managed to salvage, and what sort of ties (personal as well as socio-economic) held it together.

Comparing different concentration camps and the different periods in the history of each of them, we can distinguish: (a) the worst situations when the middle levels of power were occupied by a group of prisoner-criminals emotionally insensitive to the situation of other people; (b) situations when a closed national group took over that power and acted only to rescue its own; (c) situations when political prisoners won the upper hand (as a united group) from the start of the camp's operation and in spite of the circumstances strove to put into practice ordinary human values (e.g., the beginning of the women's camp at Majdanek); (d) situations when a group of organized and organizing political prisoners won power gradually and, conscious of its goals and methods of resistance (such as the Poles in the men's camp at Auschwitz), was capable of creating inner unity and then of breaking through the national barriers to create a common movement of resistance.

In analyzing the struggle for power in Auschwitz it is worthwhile distinguishing different phases. The first had the characteristics of a free-enterprise, "buddy" system and consisted in taking advantage of every opportunity, no matter how small, and forming small islands where life was easier than for other prisoners. In the next phase communication developed between these islands along with various forms of cooperation; pressure groups arose, capable of influencing those prisoner-functionaries who had submitted completely to their SS superiors and whose actions brought harm to the other prisoners. And with this the prisoners further extended their influence to having a say in the filling of camp functions with prisoners who were capable of resistance. At a certain point the stage was set for the operation of an organized resistance movement, which had already acquired a certain influence inside all the separate subcamps. The mechanisms of self-defense began to function, not only in the formal structure of the resistance movement but also through the energetic behavior of informal prisoner groups loyally cooperating with each other. In spite of the continuing terror and violence, a unique double authority became operative, as a result of which prisoners in a certain area (though a relatively small one) were able to resist.

Outside help—contacts with the resistance movement outside the camp and with the population who lived in the vicinity—was part of the odds favoring the resistance movement, as was the awareness that the era of concentration camps had to end, regardless of who would be granted individual survival. The vision of another life—a free, normal life—injected energy.

This firm support in the sphere of values does not change the fact that a good many prisoners at Auschwitz survived because of the camp market, because they could "talk business" with people who had lost all traits of humanity, who came not only from the ranks of criminal-prisoners, but also from the SS. Some of the prisoners who had come to the camp as felons or disturbed persons, as well as those whom the camp had transformed into a criminal element, were open to all forms of bribery. Many of them did not think that the camps would ever cease to exist or that they would be freed; they lost the perspective of a different life. Their world was unfolding in Auschwitz and they intended to take full advantage of prosperity such as they had, perhaps, never known in their normal life. They lived from day to day, creating high standards of consumption. Women in the same category would collect elegant wardrobes, an absurd activity in the camp situation. These prisoner-functionaries, privileged not to wear camp attire, would organize their own sort of fashion-show and were ready to permit any infringement as the price of a smart rag. Those rags could buy rescue for quite a few people.

A corruptible guard, or an SS officer who represented a higher authority (and thus offered more possibilities), was often very useful for the prisoners' organized resistance. They could "sell" their real knowledge about dangers within the camp and about the political situation; they could supply medicine for a price, send uncensored letters, falsify documents which were dangerous to a prisoner; they would even furnish a radio receiver and sell a weapon. Business deals carried on with persons in the administrative offices of the camp could be very dangerous in their consequences for the prisoners who arranged them. At the same time, however, if the deals were successful—and especially if they became permanent arrangements—ever greater gaps occurred in the precise mechanism of the machinery of terror.

That machinery, tended scrupulously by "honest," incorruptible SS officials, functioned without respite; except that during the period when many demoralized representatives of authority believed that a unique, never-to-be repeated opportunity to acquire a fortune had presented itself some cogs in that machinery functioned considerably less efficiently, which had great importance in the life of every prisoner.

The business arrangements which made many SS officials dependent on prisoners had further consequences: there were cases where the sense of community with other SS colleagues clearly broke down and confidence in a prisoner (or prisoners) known from everyday contacts took its place. A drunken SS officer (male or female) would set a prisoner on watch to look out for the approach of another SS officer and then go to bed for the duration of the working day to regain his energy for the next night's drunken binge. Some SS officials began to talk to "their" prisoners, who more than once managed to put a damper on the official's designs or dispose him favorably toward their own plans. Thanks to situations such as these, unsupervised time could be used to the benefit of prisoners. Under the "protection" of such an SS official, a prisoner could also manage to penetrate to another subcamp to make a necessary contact, transmit information, or deliver a parcel. In circumstances so exceptionally favorable to the prisoners, an SS official changed for a while from an authority into a conscious or unconscious tool of the prisoners'

resistance. In order to register the full truth, it must be emphasized that cases of compassion and unselfish aid did occur among
the criminal prisoners filling camp functions and even among SS
officers. The prisoners with green triangles operated under pressure from their SS bosses, but also under the increasing pressure
of opinion from the political prisoners. The SS officers in Auschwitz functioned as members of a single task force. The function
of social opinion in their case was to confirm their sense of the
new division into "human" and "nonhuman" beings and to
confirm the sense that the concentration camp was a "legitimate"
institution. Under these conditions every human gesture, every
bit of help given to a prisoner, expressed a choice of humanist
values, and therefore a condemnatory outlook on that criminal
activity in which they were participating. Such gestures were
important not only for the mechanism of resistance, but also for
the feelings of those prisoners who came into contact with them.
An SS official who had not been demoralized or one who retained
a capacity to respond in a human way became an ally of the
prisoners. His disinterested breaking of the camp regulations
increased the chances of survival for those prisoners who were
directly subject to his authority. However, he behaved in this way
only when he was outside of the immediate control of the milieu
to which he belonged.

It is difficult to evaluate responsibly how much these manifestations of compassion bore testimony to the fact that even in the
most corrupt persons some sort of humanist values had been
saved, and how much such behavior grew out of a reaction to the
fortunes of war, to the ever more numerous—as time went by—
symptoms of Nazism's defeat. Both interpretations appear justified.

CHAPTER TEN

The Organized Resistance Movement

> *Our values in the world—love, simplicity, order, the recognition*
> *of the rights of another man, the conceiving of his existence not*
> *as plunder or as a labor force, but as a field of aliveness to*
> *which we assent and desire to help—are the dikes raised against*
> *an incessantly threatening sea. The recognition of values is*
> *itself a structural part of that dike. . . . Their recognition is an*
> *acquired social habit and as such a fragile one. . . . Without*
> *care, without a human hand to pack down the patch of eroded*
> *ground, everything that is valuable will crumble away.*
>
> Jan Strzelecki, Proofs of Testimony

THE EXISTENCE and functioning of conspiratorial organizations in Auschwitz constitutes a separate chapter in the battle against Nazism—a battle carried on by the subjugated in conditions of the most oppressive discrimination.[1] The underground organizations in Nazi-occupied countries operated in situations where they ran the risk of being exposed

1. Numerous writings devoted to these matters provide detailed accounts of the activities of the resistance groups at Auschwitz; e.g., Barbara Dziubińska, "Ruch oporu w obozie masowej zagłady w Oświęcimiu," *Wojskowy Przegląd Historyczny*, no. 3 (1965); Tadeusz Hołuj, "Ludność oświęcimska i ruch oporu w obozie," *Za Wolność i Lud*, no. 4 (1956); Franciszek Kobielski, "Kontakty z obozem," *Zeszyty Oświęcimskie*, no. 5 (1961); Jerzy Łukowski, "Ruch oporu w obozie koncentracyjnym Oświęcim-Brzezinka," *Przegląd Historyczny*, no. 3 (1967); Czesław Ostankiewicz, "Konspiracyjna działalność kulturalna w Oświęcimiu," *Tygodnik Powszechny*, no. 44 (1961); Jan Wolny, "O organizowaniu pomocy lekarsko-sanitarnej w obozie kobiecym w Brzezince," *Przegląd Lekarski*, no. 1 (1965); Ludwik Rajewski, *Ruch oporu w polskiej literaturze obozowej* (Warsaw, 1971).

for their activities, of arrest and deportation to concentration camps. The clandestine organization in Auschwitz existed under conditions of acute and immediate danger; it had to adapt the forms of its activity to constant terror and to be capable of using whatever loopholes existed in the network of constant control. The structure of the conspiracy at Auschwitz required of its members, besides much caution and forethought, an understanding of the mechanism of camp terror and a knowledge of its weakest points. Previous experience in conspiratorial work was indispensable in Auschwitz, because proven models of operation had to be adapted to different conditions. The ordinary participant in the camp resistance movement had to follow as best he could two contradictory injunctions; to act with deliberate forethought, observing the rules of the conspiracy to the letter, and to be able to run the highest risks in vital situations. Every assignment had to be performed with full awareness of numerous dangers, while choosing a method to accomplish it that would minimize the danger. These rules, known in principle, but not always practiced in all underground organizations, took on a special significance in Auschwitz.

Conspiratorial organizations in Auschwitz were closely linked to clandestine organizations outside the camp and historians will have to give their views (as precisely as the documents that have been preserved will allow) on how the foundations of organized conspiracy in the camp were laid. Conclusions as to the kind of ideological and political goals that were reached as a result of links to the outside can certainly be drawn from the results. For a prisoner taking part in the resistance, the aim of conspiracy was above all the saving of prisoners' lives by whatever means possible in the camp and the signalling of SOS wherever that international call for help could be transmitted. Since the possibility of rescue was problematical, it was also a matter of bearing witness to Nazi crimes before the world and before history.

The decisive role in the resistance movement at Auschwitz was played by Poles. There were several reasons for this. Poland was a country where a large portion of the society took part in, or at least cooperated with, conspiratorial organizations; these had begun to function immediately after the Nazi takeover in 1939. Among the many thousands of Polish prisoners at Auschwitz, experienced activists of the resistance movement were relatively numerous. That Auschwitz was situated on Polish territory (and the Poles living in the vicinity of Auschwitz were not all deported) gave to prisoners of Polish nationality the best chance to make contacts outside the camp; and to the conspiratorial organizations in Poland it gave the best chance to get through to their imprisoned comrades. At the same time the organizational structure of some of the clandestine groups advocating Polish independence [e.g., the Polish Home Army] enabled information to be transmitted to countries or territories not occupied by the Nazis.

Transports from the same prisons brought to the camp groups of people who could trust each other, having come through similar experiences and tests of endurance in extreme situations. But the organizations in camp did not expand solely by means of acquaintanceships tested in prison and in the camp but also on the basis of continuity with a prisoner's previous participation in the resistance movement. The special thing about that continuity was that people who often could have been divided previously by their membership in various organizations and by their ideological differences joined up with the same camp organization. All these previous lines of division lost their definition in the face of the necessity for common defense.

It is very hard to draw the line between the spontaneous and the organized resistance movement in Auschwitz, even for those who belonged to a conspiratorial organization. For a member at the lowest level in one of the camp organizations, it was hard to say on whose behalf he was carrying out his particular instructions. Memory and the very fragmentary documents distort these past events. Doubtless they will never enable all the phenomena of conspiratorial work in the camp to be established with complete precision, much less the phenomena of spontaneous resistance among people loyally working together in response to specific situations. As it appears from the incomplete documents, the Polish organization that consolidated the resistance of political prisoners in the men's camp at Auschwitz I was the earliest to take shape. Only later did an international organization come into being. For certain, the activities of the organized resistance consisted in establishing all contacts with organizations outside the camp and transmitting documents through them that communicated what was going on in the camp; also, the collecting, transferring and delivering of these documents were organized activities, as were the frequently successful destruction or falsification of documents directly threatening to the life of individual prisoners. Their activities also included operations requiring great skill and coordination on the part of their members living in the various subcamps: such as, for example, the planning of a strategy for defense in the event of all-out danger,[2] or the revolt of the *Sonderkommando*—long in preparation but prematurely set in motion—that resulted in the destruction of two crematories and an attempted mass escape.[3] The same coordination and careful preparatory work (which required making connections with local residents and conspiratorial organizations outside the camp) were also indispensable for arranging escapes from the camp.[4] Information concerning the existence and functions of the Nazi concentration camp, including partial lists of prisoners, was transmitted to countries not occupied by the Nazis, thanks to the activity of the camp organizations. Red Cross intervention and the packages streaming into the camp in response to that information[5] sowed panic among the planners and administrators of the extermination camps, because their strictly secret operation had been exposed.

2. Reference is to the plan to kill all prisoners of the camp.
3. See, for example, Olga Wormser, "Bunt Sonderkommando w Oświęcimiu," *Widnokręgi* (1959).
4. See, for example, Tomasz Adamski, *Ucieczki oświęcimskie*, 2d ed. (Warsaw, 1969); and Tadeusz Iwaszko, "Ucieczki więźniów z obozu koncentracyjnego Oświęcim," *Zeszyty Oświęcimskie*, no. 7 (1963).
5. See Stanisław Kłodziński, "Paczki Międzynarodowego Czerwonego Krzyża dla więźniów Oświęcimia," *Przegląd Lekarski*, no. 1 (1967).

But there was still the whole great network of mutual aid, communication and information, which was partly the outgrowth of decisions and strategies coordinated by the conspiratorial organizations operating in the camp, but even more, perhaps, the consequence of spontaneous human reactions, individual strategies, and the loyal, informal cooperation of the prisoners who had the possibility of participating in this system. Delivery of medicines and extra food to the hospital barracks was accomplished not only as a result of the efforts of the camp organization, but also as a result of individual ingenuity and opportunity. The organized conspiratorial system of communication between the individual subcamps, the barracks, and the work crews supplemented "private" communication, which consisted in taking advantage of various points of contact between the otherwise isolated groups of prisoners for the purpose of transmitting oral information, smuggled written messages, and political news.

Warnings of danger threatening specific persons or groups were often due to the work of a competent organization but, many times, accidental "leaks" of information from SS officials were also responsible for them. The prisoners who "intercepted" that information immediately sought out other prisoners who could relay the information to the threatened person. Information concerning impending selections, transports, staff changes in the SS, or reprisals was disseminated through the organized as well as the informal information system. Contact with local residents living in the vicinity of the camp was also part of both systems of resistance.

Sabotage had relatively little meaning in Auschwitz I and Auschwitz II-Birkenau. Most of the prisoners performed senseless activities or activities connected with the everyday life of the camp community. The slower work tempo served the purpose of biological survival above all, and as such was practiced and exhorted by all who understood the camp mechanism. The prisoners completed the German motto on the gate to the camp—"*Arbeit macht frei*" ["Work will set you free"]—with the words "to go up the chimney,"[6] thus creating a popular saying which warned prisoners that work was a method of hastening death. Other motivations accompanied the sabotaging of work by prisoners who were employed in factories producing for the German weapons industry (e.g., Auschwitz III-Buna Monowice).

The planning and organizing by the "Auschwitz Group" of international cooperation among prisoners who would work together in the same organization for a common purpose paralleled the rise of informal camp groups made up of individuals of different nationalities. National barriers which acted as such a critical obstacle in the anonymous and multilingual crowd were cleared at various levels of cooperation among individuals sleeping on the same "roost" or working in the same crew. These antagonisms were overcome above all thanks to members of the intelligentsia, who realized that it was necessary to work together and that antipathies are usually irrational; such persons made use of their knowledge of foreign languages to alleviate conflict and to enlist loyal cooperation.

The male prisoners' protection of the women imprisoned at Auschwitz-Birkenau from the brutality of female prisoner-functionaries was sometimes the result of organized activity, but mostly it fell into the category of spontaneous, individual help. Often prisoners who were cooperating in an organized action that served to protect prisoners did not even know they were performing their specific task within the framework of a centralized system of resistance.

To explain the complicated structure of the resistance movement, it should be discussed in terms of activities that were to varying degrees structured. The camp organizations functioned as structured groups. As a rule their members possessed only enough information to carry out their assigned task. If the task required wider cooperation, they enlisted the help of prisoners

6. The saying meant that exhaustion from overwork would send you to the gas chamber, into the crematory oven and up the chimney in the form of smoke.— TRANS.

who were subordinate to them in the structure of the organization, informing them that they were acting on orders from the organization; they also enlisted the help of the most trusted prisoners who did not belong to the organization, telling them only what was necessary to perform the task. Sometimes they had to make use of the services of other prisoners whom they did not fully trust, but who—because of the function they performed in camp—were indispensable to the successful accomplishment of the task. In such situations the request for help was justified by the need for a friendly service, or was supported by material argument.

So too, in everyday camp conditions in the individual barracks and work crews, situations arose that required close cooperation on the basis of fast, direct aid. A steadily improving communication system between "old timers" and relatively adapted prisoners made it possible to react more and more quickly to such situations. Prisoners who because of functions performed were allowed to circulate within one subcamp, or who were allowed to pass into other subcamps with their work crews, took part in the communication system (not only in the sense of transmitting information, but also of supplying medicines, clothes, and food). A prisoner who because of the work he performed was allowed to make various contacts within his own subcamp, but especially if he was able to do so in other subcamps, acquired valuable acquaintances. He could become an intermediary for prisoners signalling a need and seeking help from others who could give it. Prisoners working in crews which gave access to information or necessities of life joined the network of mutual services that functioned alongside the commodity market system of exchanges or sales. Through this network of individual contacts, the actions of a spontaneous resistance movement were conceived and carried out. The members of the organized resistance took part in this spontaneous activity as well, but in a different role—the role of obliging fellow-prisoners making the most of opportunities.

Along with spontaneous actions that served directly to save a life, "leisure activities" arose just as spontaneously within groups of prisoners transported from the same jail or working in crews that frequently came in contact. According to personal connections and interests, these activities could be discussion groups or literary evenings in which a prisoner knowing poetry and literature well could recite poems or relate the classics, or gatherings to listen to a recital by famous singers or naturally-talented prisoners; or they could be parties dreamed up on the spot by one of the prisoners. Any idea would do that—if only for a short time—transported one to another world, allowed for complete detachment from the environment and for "playing pre-camp roles." Hours or evenings such as these provided food for thought and oiled the mechanism of mental detachment; in the conditions at Auschwitz, however, they were among the rarest of occurrences and very few prisoner groups took part in them.

There was also a permanent, relatively organized system of political information at work. Those prisoners with access to the sources of information were the transmitters, and the information circulated informally around all the subcamps. This communication involved a selection: depending on the situation at the battle fronts and on the opportunities for getting through to different sources, the information that was communicated was either true or false, but as a rule it was something that sustained hopes for a swift end to the war and for surviving the camp.

The next rung down in the hierarchy of these activities, with respect to the lesser degree of their organization, were all types of spontaneous forms of aid and cooperation rendered to one's fellows in very difficult situations, such as the concealment of the weakest in the middle of a row of prisoners (the ends of every row were very exposed to beatings), taking the place of the weakest prisoner at work, giving him the warmest clothes, sharing food. To this category of activity also belong all the techniques of buoying up those prisoners who had lost their reserves of mental endurance. This meant releasing the tension in dangerous situations through humor, the telling of stories, a song, a laugh, recollections, plans for the future; it meant finding the most varied subjects or games to distract attention from the present.

Every proof of loyalty and sympathy, every hour of a shared life of the imagination (personal as well as historical) every moment of laughter, every joke was part of the arsenal of collective defense and thus an element of the resistance movement. Finally there were the situations in which a prisoner through inner dialogue sought within himself the strength to resist. His own further endurance depended on the course of these dialogues, as did his capacity for cooperation with his fellow prisoners.

Not only in the reminiscences of former inmates of the camp, but also in discussions on related subjects, the need crops up to make value judgments—to assign degrees of guilt and degrees of merit. Belonging to the resistance movement and being active as an organizer is usually treated in categories of high merit. If these matters are analyzed in sociological terms, such judgments must be viewed in relation to the prisoner's place in the camp's structure of violence. Depending on that place, a gesture of compassion made to a fellow prisoner in the same (the worst) situation could be much harder and demand greater energy than participation in a bold and important operation of the underground organization. Mostly prisoners who stood higher in the camp hierarchy belonged to this organization; they were better nourished, had a lighter workload, and performed various camp functions. Regardless of how difficult it had been for them earlier and how long they had fought for their lives in the most oppressive conditions, at the moment when they became capable of taking part in a coordinated action their circumstances were relatively stable (in camp terms). They were not starved to the point of losing their capacity for action, cooperation, and defense. It is certainly to their great credit that they did not use their place in this hierarchy solely for their individual survival, but risked that place and their life in order to help other prisoners. However, many prisoners would surely have done the same in better conditions and having the same possibilities.

Being part of the camp resistance movement was the greatest privilege. Along with the higher place in the camp hierarchy, thanks to which one's chances of survival were increased, went the awareness of participation in a battle. A member of a camp organization was no longer just a hunted animal, but in his own mind became a complete human person, doing battle with criminals. Regardless of how unequal the two sides of the battle, the very consciousness of being able to resist, to cooperate, to participate in rescuing others created a mental climate that in the camp conditions was a luxury of the spirit. There was also the awareness of support from an organized structure inside the camp and the awareness of cooperation with those who were fighting in freedom.

The battle for value has different dimensions. One can evaluate it on a scale of results and by the measure of energy needed to take part in it. The objective consequences of organized resistance were certainly greater for the rescue of prisoners than the results of solitary efforts.

To fully evaluate the crucial significance of camp organizations in the battle for human life and basic values and their large role in aiding prisoners, one must (viewing actions in relation to situations) acknowledge the greatness of thousands of anonymous actions and gestures. In hopeless situations stepping forward in defense of another person regardless of the reprisals to which the defender exposed himself was very rarely effective. The victory that he carried off was won in another dimension: in the world of values.

Irrespective of the level of organization on which the prisoners' resistance movement operated, or how it asserted itself in the context of concrete situations, it was responsible for the rescue of all those who survived the camp. There is not one survivor who did not find support and help among fellow prisoners. No one could have survived on his own physical and mental strength. The majority of those who perished also experienced such aid, if it was at all possible.

Every manifestation of resistance, even though reprisals (and guilt by association) threatened those who took part in it, cracked the structure of terror, proved to those who had lost hope that hope existed, showed that there were indeed ways out of a dead-end situation, and they were various. Every method of opposition—no matter whether it increased the survival odds for a group of prisoners or a particular person, or was the immediate cause of death for the resister—expressed a protest against violence.

Every manifestation of loyalty and cooperation was proof that terror liberates the strength to resist and produces attitudes of self-reliance. This self-reliance was expressed not only through the struggle for life but also through independent choice of the type of death. This struggle for life and self-reliance was also waged in the sphere of values. Every gesture of loyalty, of sympathy, and of organized resistance was an externalization and a defense of the basic values of European civilization against the terrorism of those who denied the existence of those values.

It is hard to say whether this resistance would have been possible in the conditions at Auschwitz had there not existed that frame of reference, those fighting nations of Europe. This common system of values united prisoners and their nations and strengthened their resistance, thanks to the sense of support. The Germans who resisted the turning of their government into a terroristic Nazi gang during the period 1933–39 did not have such support.

CHAPTER ELEVEN

Mechanisms of Adaptation and Self-Defense

> *. . . human life involves values which have little to do with biological needs and which transcend the survival of individual persons.*
>
> René Dubos, Man Adapting

S OCIOLOGICAL STUDIES of animals have shown that, among herds living in freedom in their natural habitat, not only relationships inside the herd, but also relationships with other herds are governed by manners and "a code of chivalry." For example, a deer that wins a duel does not kill his rival; the defeated performs a symbolic gesture and withdraws a customary distance. Experimental research has shown that the forced overcrowding of animal herds in a confined space, unsuited to their needs, causes total anarchy: "chivalrous" conduct gives way to a vicious and ruthless struggle for survival, dominance, and living space.

The Social Experiment

The concentration camp constituted a unique social experiment carried out on human beings. The basic difference consists in the fact that the sociologists experimenting on animals were testing the action of only one factor. the confinement of living space, while the Nazi experiment involved the application of a whole range of negative stimuli. Nazism made use of an extensive social technology for the manipulation of human beings, correctly assuming (for the most part) that a specific set of conditions and stimuli ought to bring about the projected social responses. A body of socio-technological knowledge underlay the concept of training accomplices and executors of crimes; it supplied the data for the application of various methods of terror, and as a comprehensive system it was employed for the realization of the concept of concentration camps.

The methods of social engineering based on this knowledge and used in the training of Nazi young people, who were ready to act as tools of crime, achieved all the anticipated results. To a very serious degree they coerced into obedience, or even brought about the willing acceptance, of large segments of the German nation. They were also responsible for the total demoralization of a small proportion of prisoners in the concentration camps, the partial emotional deadening of the majority of prisoners, and serious social malfunctions in the prisoners' environment.

Social engineering enabled the machinery of death to be set in motion on a mass scale in the countries defeated by Hitler's armies and especially in Nazi prisons and concentration camps. It turned out to be deceptive, however, in the area of psychological terror, which was supposed to bring about the willing acceptance of force as a higher value or at least coerce into passive obedience all the societies to which that technique was applied.

The Nazi "social experiment" was not scientifically controlled; the activities conducted were analyzed only for their effectiveness with respect to set tasks.

It now seems possible to think of Auschwitz as an ex post facto experiment.[1] In attempting to analyze the camp in such terms, one should ask what happened to people who were transplanted

1. Compare Francis S. Chapin, *Experimental Designs in Sociological Research* (New York: Harper, 1955; reprint ed., Westport, Conn.: Greenwood, 1974), chapter 5, "Ex post facto Design: From Present to Past."

into conditions offering no chances of survival, who were further-more subjected to a set of direct negative stimuli in the form of physical and mental terror and to a set of accompanying stimuli in the form of being present at the killing of others, all this in circumstances which deprived them of any chance to act effectively.

"The social experiment" conducted by Nazi gangsters in Auschwitz produced the biological results its planners antici-pated, causing rapid physical deterioration of a mass of pris-oners. This deterioration brought on mental disturbances (the result of the disease of starvation). It is no longer possible to give a precise answer to the question of how much of the behavior of individual prisoners should be interpreted in terms of a limited awareness, or even as unconscious, and how much of it as fully conscious. The extensive literature of camp reminiscences tells of much aggressive behavior directed against fellow prisoners. Investigative research into the disease of starvation at Auschwitz describes the disease's symptoms and charts its course. But to establish a diagnosis of individual behavior or mental soundness is difficult, owing to people's varying degrees of physical endur-ance. It is equally difficult to judge the degree and extent to which these stimuli caused sociopathological symptoms. And there are not enough data to establish the effects on a prisoner's mental state of such stimuli as constant danger, terror, the circumstances accompanying the crimes, and the indeterminate length of incarceration in the camp. There were many cases of acute disturbances accompanied by the classic symptoms of mental diseases. Because the concept of "mental health" is an imprecise one, perhaps it can be stated that besides the obvious cases of mental disease various kinds of mental disturbances also took place, along with a decline of endurance in the nervous system, and that to varying degrees the symptoms of these dis-turbances were observable.

So too we have no right to pronounce whether the cases of the majority of extremely aggressive actions violating previously rec-ognized social norms constitute an analogy to an animal herd forced by circumstances into a ruthless battle for existence, or, again, whether they should be interpreted in the categories of medicine and social pathology.

Certain behavior can be interpreted in terms of personality change and adaptability. The extreme cases of a total lack of adaptive mechanisms and the inability to disengage oneself from one's own biography as a free person were suicides. Between these extreme cases and the ability to adapt was a whole range of behavior. At the bottom of the scale was the group of Greek Jewish women, all of whom became *"Muselmänner,"* and about whom very little is known as a result of linguistic and cultural barriers. One can call a prisoner defensively adapted who was able to experience the camp as if it were ordinary life. Such a prisoner found in the camp not only countless failures and reasons to despair but also little and great joys (though in radically different proportions), feelings of closeness with other people, and amusing events to which he could react with humor. Out of the circumstances of his former life and his life here and now, his interests developed and his need to act arose.[2]

The forms of adaptation based on collaboration with the structure of terror have already been discussed. It is worth adding that, for many, this method of adapting was fraught with conflict. With it went either moments of awareness of one's own fall (a moral dissonance) or a growing dread as Hitler's defeat drew nearer (a cognitive dissonance, stemming from doubts over one's choice of the winning side). This type of adaptation (relatively rare as we have seen) defined the narrow field where the Nazi experiment succeeded on the psychological plane among those who identified with the aggressor.

Such categories do not apply to one-time situations in which a prisoner's psychological resistance broke down and collapsed in the face of immediate and extreme danger or under the influence of physical torture exceeding his endurance. He was not ostracized from the prisoner community because of it—his witnesses

2. See the literature of camp reminiscences, especially S. Grzesiuk, *Pięć lat kacetu*, 2d ed. (Warsaw, 1960).

understood—but his inner self-censoring mechanisms were set in motion, and they could lead either to a deep sense of guilt and self-destruction, or to the development of endurance of any form of terror. The outcome of this inner battle was, to a large degree, dependent on the attitude of his fellow-prisoners.

Judging from the immediate results of Hitler's "social experiment," it can be stated that the methods of social engineering applied inside the camp brought about the biological annihilation of a majority of the prisoners, the serious physical deterioration of all prisoners, and many mental disturbances.

What doomed that experiment to fail was the fact that the Nazi mind had not considered the possibility of psychological resistance in extremity or the various forms of struggle and solidarity in self-defense.

Reduction of Material Needs

Resistance can be expressed in many ways. Not every situation affords the chance to give open battle, or even to make a passive protest. Under the circumstances at Auschwitz, maximum adaptation had to be achieved. Resistance was expressed in the constant effort to maintain inner freedom while outwardly adapting. In the battle for this freedom prisoners gave each other mutual assistance. Each person alone, however, decided where to set the limits on his inner freedom. To expand these limits meant a struggle to increase not only the endurance of a weak organism but also mental endurance.

This struggle was most intense on the level of the simplest matters—matters essential to individual existence, as well as to living and working with others in the same situation. The Auschwitz motto of resistance in its simplest form was: "Let's not give in." It meant nothing more than to try to survive, to try to adapt to conditions as they were. The necessary corollary had to be: reduce material needs to their ultimate limits—but those limits bore not the remotest likeness to what economists conceive of as "basic needs." This was a matter of accepting with humor the leap into a misty past, a matter of wrenching oneself out of civilized habits of sleeping, sitting, eating, washing, dressing, attending to physiological needs. It meant calmly foregoing the cultural behavior which requires the utilization of a set of objects considered indispensable by modern man (regardless of his financial circumstances). A prisoner's first set of weapons consisted of a couple of pieces of ill-fitting garments and horrible wooden clogs that forced him to relearn how to walk. The lucky ones owned their own bowl and spoon and also a scrap of soap. This situation could be traumatic, but if taken with good humor it could provoke a laugh.

From the start one had to accept the taste of the camp "diet" and the unsanitary conditions that surrounded the production and distribution of food. Those who could not manage to do this in the first days of their stay were surrendering to external force; they suffered premature loss of physical strength and psychological stamina. The existing conditions also required adjustment of the need for personal cleanliness. In the sanitary conditions of the women's camp at Auschwitz-Birkenau, this meant fighting for access to water or foregoing part of the liquid meant for drinking in favor of basic hygiene. It also meant fighting insects at every free moment. Sleeping was a collective activity that required adherence to certain rules on the part of the inhabitants crowded on one "roost." It was a matter of making the most of the space as well as mutual protection from the cold.

Inner resistance took various forms. One could eat the desired piece of bread immediately. Or one could, though feeling hungry, keep part of it in one's pocket, conscious of freedom won: I am not eating it all, because I choose not to. This form of self-defense, however, was related to the tolerance of hunger, which varies widely among individuals. The prisoner who managed (with humor and calmness, or relative calmness) to accept the reduction of his material needs in the first days was capable, later on, of adding to his arsenal. Every piece of string acquired, every scrap of handkerchief, every needle or nail were things that enriched the prisoners' cultural environment.

The next stage of adaptation depended on a prisoner's relation to his work in the camp. Regardless of accompanying circumstances, a prisoner's first jobs were usually nasty and oppressive. Most prisoners began their career hauling sewage. In this situation, the camp motto stood for innovation and improvement of technique. The method of loading the wagon had to give the impression of lifting a great weight, the stance while pushing it had to suggest great physical effort. It was essential to conquer one's disgust at the smell emitted by the load. The discovery that performing this job gave one the privilege of physical inviolability was cause for rejoicing. Such was the stench of the crews working in the sewers removing sewage that SS officials, instead of reacting "normally," ran off holding their noses and yelling: "*Scheisskommando schneller.*" [Shitgang, hurry up!] The conclusion to be drawn was clear: the *Scheisskommando* was relatively seldom exposed to beatings and searches, and this created further practical opportunities for adapting to the camp.

One important weapon of inner resistance that could not be taken away was a prisoner's sense of humor. Mainly, games had to be naive and primitive. Those who hauled sewage could pretend to be horses. The crew's horsy sounds and behavior would draw the overseer, a German prostitute, into the game, which suited her level, and she would change from dangerous camp official into a harmless wagon-driver. A sense of humor was also a salvation in dangerous situations. Sometimes a whispered quip could bring release from the paralysis of fear. Everyone who refused to "give in" had his own defense mechanisms. The sight of a raging SS officer became less menacing as soon as one imagined him with his pants down or lying drunk in the mud.

Feelings of strength also came from spontaneous, uncoordinated reactions to great danger. Among the inmates of one barracks who were standing in an all-night penal roll call, a rumor started to the effect that the punishment would end with a selection for the gas chamber. When dawn broke over the rows of tormented women, tottering from fatigue, it brought to light the bits of brick and the stones (some small, some heavy) lying ready to be used for their self-defense.

Prisoners who similarly survived this first stage of adaptation won the chance to improve the conditions of their existence. They began to understand for themselves the laws of camp life, and to a certain extent they could predict what infractions of the rules were worth committing, and also when and under what circumstances one could afford to do so with the least risk. They began to understand that obedience was equivalent to a death sentence, while disobedience was a postponement.

The possibility and the type of risk-taking, as well as the scale of the risks, were all determined by the prisoner's place in the camp structure, by the type of work he did, the extent of his social connections with other prisoners, the network of relationships connecting smaller and larger prisoner groups. A prisoner's adaptation depended not only on his acceptance of camp conditions and controlling his fear of camp authorities; it also depended on his ability to get along with other prisoners who constituted a huge collective of various nationalities, classes and cultures, with various character formations and attitudes, lifestyles and levels of cultivation. It required the utmost tolerance of shortcomings or "otherness." To aggression one had to be able to react effectively by attempting to understand or by making a joke. To a vulgar but friendly gesture one had to react with kindness and not take offense. To extreme pessimism one had to respond with optimism. One also needed the ability to alleviate the inevitable conflicts and misunderstandings due to the language barriers and to the different cultural interpretations of the same behavior. There was also the necessity to bring anyone who weakened the solidarity of a group back into line.

To be accepted by a group of fellow-prisoners, one needed certain traits of character that eased the process of living together: friendliness, readiness to help, patience, tolerance, self-control, boldness and decisiveness in protecting the weak, quick reflexes and a sense of humor. One also needed certain abilities that were helpful for organizing life in the camp or to turn the attention of one's companions to matters unconnected with the camp.

A prisoner whose attitude won the confidence and acceptance of a larger group of inmates gained another weapon. He was bolstered by the collective strengths of the group who gave him support and to whom he gave support.

Regardless of a prisoner's talents for living and working in common with others, in certain matters he was a solitary protagonist. The process of adapting to external circumstances could not stop at the point where life was still the only frame of reference for action, imagination, and social behavior. Yet one more step—that very difficult step "into the dark"—separated him from complete adaptation (in a positive sense). The landscape of death surrounding the prisoners produced a different outlook on that inevitability.

Much has been written about the so-called callousness of concentration-camp prisoners. Apparently the process of hardening followed various courses and produced diverse psychological effects. There is no point in giving a psychological description of these diverse mental processes—they depend so much on the individual personality and on the specific situations encountered—but the two basic variants are worth distinguishing.

Insensitivity could arise as a result of viewing death daily. Such sights were a "normal" part of camp life and to the prisoners they became as commonplace as familiar objects observed day-in and day-out. The emotional connection was lost between a human person and a dead body that cannot suffer; a corpse became one of many emotionally neutral objects. Emotional callousness in such a case consisted in dehumanizing human remains. This process did not, however, immunize the imagination against one's own death. Rather, in moments of weakness, it could evoke a feeling of envy toward that form of escape from the camp.

Desensitization could also occur on a philosophical plane. A dynamic desire to live could coexist with a philosophical consent to one's own death. In this gamble for life over which the prisoners had no influence, fate, like a roulette ball, would come to rest on the black or on the red—the red meant living to see the end of the Nazi era and realizing one's dreams of a normal life; the black meant the end of one's own life and the chance for others to survive. With such an attitude toward one's own death, insensitivity did not consist in dehumanizing dead bodies, but in being aware that all fates, including one's own, were a gamble. Such an attitude could bring one to a playful outlook on one's own death and it liberated the deepest levels of camp humor. While observing the shapes of the chimney smoke from the crematory, and without losing one's identification with those who died, one might envision little angels in flight and imagine the shape that one would take oneself at the appropriate time. Such a defense mechanism helped to lessen the camp terrors and the feeling of guilt toward those who perished, as it also set a limit to Nazi power: what more can you do to me—I'll fly out through the chimney. So what?

Such an outlook did not mean passively giving up the chance to survive—on the contrary, it released new defense mechanisms and by creating a certain distance from death it reduced the threat.

The desensitizing process changed one's relationship to the fact of death. But the reactions to dying were much more complex, especially if it was accompanied by brutality and great physical suffering. In these situations the most powerful mechanisms of self-defense sometimes let one down. At this point the possibilities to adapt usually came to an end.

Each relatively adapted prisoner created his own psychological mechanisms to protect himself from feeling totally unfree. He fought for his inner freedom and used various means to expand its limits. In this difficult battle for inner freedom a prisoner's priceless ally was his imagination. It enabled him to detach himself from life in the camp and transported him to the free world of dreams, and that world was the prisoner's personal property which could not be plundered. His imagination also helped him to acquire an historical perspective. He could transport himself to distant times, identifying with the slave living in a barbaric country and feeling a common bond with all who, throughout the history of mankind, have lived at the bottom of the social hierarchy. The strength of his imagination was able to carry him out of the nightmare surrounding him and into another world. Each one created his own inner world and let it expand. Sometimes in that inner reality one managed to find a refuge from camp reality. In spite of the yearning for loved ones who remained outside in freedom, the awareness that they were relatively safe gave one strength. For those who did not have such knowledge, it was harder to find inner strength.

A prisoner could seek to establish a distance between himself and the camp hierarchy in many ways. He could view those with authority over prisoner's lives as a primitive gang, or as a different species, who by representing physical force revealed their psychological and moral nothingness. The sense of the superiority of one's own values enabled one (in moments of relative calm) to construct a social hierarchy in which ascendancy (or the lack of it) was not determined by the place in the power structure but by the place in the hierarchy of values.

Religious faith could also be of help in finding this distance, as could other convictions based on a worldview in which humanist values predominated. Every prisoner more or less consciously carried on an inner battle on the plane of values. Along with that battle, regardless of one's opinion of the odds for individual survival, went the profound conviction that (regardless of the dimensions of physical strength) humanist values would triumph. The vision of inevitable defeat for a gang that was breaking every fundamental moral norm and the vision of a punishment for the crimes they committed arose constantly in the minds of prisoners and furnished a subject for many discussions.

The psychological processes leading to inner freedom liberated a perspectivist imagination—various visions of a free world where no man would use force over another. Concentration-camp prisoners were never under the illusion that the conditions surrounding them constituted an "abuse of power"; those conditions were legitimated by administrative orders, orders given by the Nazi government. They had to view both party and government as participants in the creation of the camp, and therefore as belonging to the category of criminals and felons. Resistance in the camp took shape not as an attitude toward a foreign country that emerged victorious from the first stage of the war, but as an attitude toward all forms of perverted authority that under the guise of law perpetrate criminal activity.

CHAPTER TWELVE

People and Values

*We the living carry death within—only our thoughts enliven
the dead. We are, and then we're gone; we were, and now
we're gone; we will yet be, and then be gone.*

*May all people die young though their hair be white and
their faces furrowed by joy and sorrow. May they die at home—
if home was their world. May they die in battle—if their life
was battle. May they die like flaming torches—if their life was
sacrifice. May they die loving what they loved most—believing
in what they believed. May they never lose the hope that people
shall not die in suffering.*

A.P.

I N T O A U S C H W I T Z were herded people with specific needs
and habits, and who had been reared in the moral traditions
of their nations, their ideological groups, and their social
milieus. The scale of such differentiation markedly exceeded any
to which an average person could be exposed during his entire
lifetime. Full understanding of all these differences colliding with
each other on the crowded premises of the concentration camp
would require anthropological studies of at least the entire area
of Europe and any attempts to simplify these problems are bound
to fail.

For this reason it seems safer to limit further discussion to the
Polish national group, on the assumption that the majority of
conclusions pertain to the prisoners as a whole, regardless of
what cultural system shaped them, or of what values were instilled by their milieu in the process of their upbringing, or of
what authorities uphold the moral standards they recognized.

Values as a Frame of Reference

The decided majority of Polish society in the period 1939–45 had been brought up in the traditions of patriotism and Christianity. The values instilled by this training were at the bottom of many spontaneous reactions. The cult of strength was foreign to these traditions. Religious standards provided the imperative of caring for the weak. Both national and religious traditions shaped Polish reactions of resistance to force, to all forms of brutality, and to the destruction of those values around which Polish society had consolidated.

The concepts of "command" and "obedience," whose over-positive valuation so tragically weighed on the German nation, were for Poles morally neutral words. Only in context—whose command? for what purpose given? what is its content?—did the words acquire a positive or, as was the case, extremely negative moral significance. At that time Polish society still contained too many living witnesses of the partitions and too many who had taken part in the battles for Polish independence[1] for any type of collaboration to win acceptance. Resistance to the Nazi occupier intensified considerably in response to the way in which the occupation was carried out. A firm backing in historical traditions and an unequivocal judgment as to the values of force constituted the strength of the Resistance, a strength which Nazi social engineering underestimated and neglected to take into account in directing operations.

In Poland that backing could not be cut off from Polish political prisoners nor from the many other Poles who ended up in concentration camps as a result of various reprisals. From the standpoint of those values, Nazi conduct in the defeated country, and especially in the concentration camp, was unequivocally perceived as criminal activity, sanctioned by the government of the Third Reich. To those who carried out these activities, the Poles reacted as to gangsters, and the common stereotype of the "German gangster" carried with it a condemnation of

1. Reference is to the generation who fought in World War I and in 1920.

those actions that were judged to be indisputably criminal. Thanks to this certitude, there was no moral hesitation over how to react. At the same time the situation of extreme terror produced in everyone the dread of finding himself in a specific situation where he would be incapable of the right reaction, and usually that fear was fully justified.

The frame of reference for every form of resistance was the system of values that were acknowledged and practiced. This value system (although modified and diminished in camp conditions) enabled many prisoners not only to survive biologically, but also to maintain their attitude of protest against force and violence in relation to the human person.

Models and values that are deeply internalized create the strength to resist every alien system which denies those values. This does not mean that these models and values could be put into action in their pure form at Auschwitz. Translated into the language of everyday camp conditions, they defined the field of each individual's battle, on which he sustained defeats as well as victories.

The Reinterpretation of Moral Standards

Were we to understand the axiom, "existence determines consciousness," in the most immediate fashion, then the existence consciously created by the founders of the concentration camp at Auschwitz—for the purpose of physically destroying and morally depraving the prisoners, for the purpose of crushing their capacity to resist by using all the means at their disposal—should have produced all the intended results. The intensive functioning of these means generated a situation in which the Nazi social experiment should have been a total success, that is, all prisoners should have changed into wild beasts in accord with the formula which yielded results in the training of Nazi youth. The pressure of depravity ought to have been even greater than among the Nazis, because the application of socio-technological knowledge was much more comprehensive and more forceful.

If the prisoners' behavior is to be evaluated from the standpoint of the highest moral principles—and only the prisoner who was loyally protected at the risk of many other prisoners' lives and at the cost of their sacrifices could maintain himself at this level—then it would have to be stated that all prisoners succumbed to savagery. They became a threatened crowd who broke moral laws, ignored social customs, used vulgar language, pushed and shoved each other, and were incapable of respecting the majesty of death.

It seems that the moral problems of Auschwitz should be approached in a different way.[2] It is obvious that a society's whole socio-economic and political structure has to affect the formation of a hierarchy of needs and values. As conditions improve, social needs grow and new cultural values appear, to which members of the society aspire.

A condition of adaptation to concentration-camp life was the reduction of needs (discussed in the previous chapter). Persons who had been sure up to that point that everything bestowed by modern civilization was necessary for life were able to adapt to the situation of primeval man, deprived of tools and weapons, weak and defenseless in the face of the surrounding environment. The highly developed system of values which was created in such a person by his upbringing clashed with a set of conditions for which that system was incongruous. Taught to honor and practice the whole set of rules stemming from civilized moral norms, the prisoners were placed in the position of having to revise their hierarchy of values. Irrespective of whether that process was initiated by an infringement of recognized norms or by a change of the content and scope of recognized norms, it yielded either a new system of diminished values that were acknowledged and

2. Another aspect of the problem of moral changes in Auschwitz is discussed extensively and in depth by A. Glińska, "Z badań nad moralnością więźniów Oświęcimia," *Przegląd Lekarski*, no. 1 (1967), pp. 37–45; A. Glińska, "Istota i mechanism przemian w moralności więźniów Oświęcimia," *Przegląd Lekarski*, no. 1 (1969), pp. 57–60; A. Glińska, "Kierunek przekształceń moralnych wśród więźniów Oświęcimia," *Przegląd Lekarski*, no. 1 (1969), pp 53–57; see also A. Glińska, "Moralność więźniów Oświęcimia," *Etyka*, vol. 2 (1967), pp. 173–232.

practiced, or discrepancies in the systems of values acknowledged and practiced.

A prisoner who made no revisions or reductions in the hierarchy of moral standards previously acknowledged had to perish if he applied them in an absolute way. Such a prisoner could only survive if he benefited from the help and care of those who infringed some of those standards or eliminated them from their system of values. A prisoner who in his mind remained faithful to his previous system of values, but in his daily living arrangements had to break them, lived with a destructive feeling of guilt, and either perished or reduced his standards in such a way as to lessen the dissonance between his convictions and his conduct.

The pattern of diminishment was similar no matter whether the process of reducing moral standards occurred on the existential or the intellectual plane and regardless of the religious or ideological values which had shaped a particular person. This pattern took the course of (1) reduction of various systems of morality to one system that countenanced those values universally recognized as the most important, (2) reinterpretation of norms so that a diminishment of their content and/or scope took place, and (3) elimination of norms that were dysfunctional in camp conditions.

The prisoners who came to Auschwitz had been shaped by various European systems of social, national, and religious values whose common attribute was humanism. The reduction process first of all eliminated the differences between these systems—the lines which divided them became unimportant. For this reason it is also of no consequence what names we give to these systems: whether we use the language of nineteenth-century moralists (who proclaimed the principle of "The greatest happiness for the greatest number"), or the language of socialism (formulated most succinctly in the mottos of the French Revolution, *"Liberté, Égalité, Fraternité,"* or the language of Christianity (whose precepts and prohibitions are formulated in the Decalogue and whose central principle is "Love your neighbor as yourself"). Regardless of what moral authority these norms exerted and which of these formulations shaped the attitudes of different prisoners, the norms had to succumb to further reduction, depending on specific situations, just as the prisoner's elementary material needs underwent curtailment.

Conditions of extremity compel one to choose what is most important. That which was most important turned out to be something common to all ideologies, religions, and moralities. Out of vast cultural complexity, out of varied value systems, emerged a spontaneous simplicity, a repeated reaction to external conditions where all subtle socio-ethical debates became pointless.

Only the person who fully understood weakness could survive and salvage his values; one needed an intelligence that was nondogmatic, that reacted flexibly to the environment, drawing the most apt conclusions from a concrete situation over which one had no control. Only such an attitude and skill enabled one to make a relevant moral choice.

Even reduced to a common denominator, systems of morality with their particular rules could not have constituted a foundation for action. These rules were a bit too radical and they were not suited to the conditions at Auschwitz. To have put them into practice in their known versions would have required heroic stances from everyone. Prisoners at Auschwitz had to be capable of creativity in the sphere of moral standards. For this reason, the voluminous literature on the subject of value systems and moral standards is relatively useless for the analysis of so misunderstood a matter (and, for many authors, so upsetting a matter) as the moral attitudes of prisoners in Nazi concentration camps.[3]

By reinterpreting the standards according to which they had been brought up and by practicing them in a necessarily diminished form, the prisoners were waging a battle on the moral plane

3. Scholarly works that treat moral problems systematically apply to societies living under normal conditions. The subtleties which are distinguished in these classifications have proven little suited for the analysis of the problems of living in Auschwitz.

with the most degenerate forms of power. Theirs was a battle in defense of those values to be saved under all circumstances.

Every norm constituting a product of culture was rendered dysfunctional. In the conditions of the concentration camp, each of the Ten Commandments required fundamental reinterpretation. The beautiful mottos of the nineteenth century had to be restated in a minimal form: "The least suffering." Only the most important of the socialist watchwords remained: "*Fraternité*," In practice, the most beautiful motto "Love your neighbor as yourself" would have required the attitude of an early Christian martyr. In the language of a prisoner battling for his values it sounded like "Do not harm your neighbor and, if at all possible, save him." He who passed through Auschwitz practicing that one rule salvaged the highest values.

The few who were able to "love their neighbor as themselves" attained the value of highest heroism. By their conduct they proved that existence did not determine consciousness: by their attitude they defied camp conditions, simultaneously reducing their material needs below the minimum.

He who under conditions of terror and coercion achieved inner freedom, at least to some extent, carried off the only form of victory possible within the existing situation. With such an attitude he disproved the doubtful theory of the need to identify with the aggressor[4] (which applies only within a certain very limited range); he expressed his solidarity with his fellow prisoners and his protest against violence. Only when he found himself in a situation that was markedly better than that of the majority of prisoners could he wage an active fight for that freedom.

In the concentration camp the socialist ideal of equality lost its meaning. In its place appeared another aspiration: to fill the higher places in a structure of inequality with persons who would protect, not murder, their fellow man.

The Decalogue had to undergo radical revision. "Do not kill,"

4. Bruno Bettelheim, "Individual and Mass Behavior in Extreme Situations," in *Readings in Social Psychology*, ed. E. Maccoby et al. (New York: Holt, Rinehart and Winston, 1958).

that fundamental human norm, only applied to those who were being killed; the relatively few cases of killing a camp assassin became legendary, for they signalled that a death sentence had been carried out on someone guilty of numerous murders and that the one who had been killed could kill no more. "Do not bear false witness against your neighbor" was radically restricted by the necessity for unified defense. If a prisoner with some chances of survival was to be severely punished or deprived of life for infringing camp regulations, then the infractions had to be blamed on a dying person, someone who was already escaping the suffering, or on a prisoner-assassin who thus lost the possibility of terrorizing others. "Do not desire your neighbor's wife, or any of his goods" was, in its second part, totally irrelevant to camp conditions in which the objects of desire were always the necessities of life, and were always the property of other people. The first part was mostly pointless, since neighbors' wives were not accessible in the closed subcamps, and besides lust was extinguished in severely starved organisms. The meaning and scope of "Do not steal" changed radically. Depending on the nature of the stolen article and where it was stolen, it was either viewed as a misdeed or highly esteemed as a moral act. To steal from a living prisoner who was in similar or worse circumstances was a deeply immoral act. All kinds of thefts that did no harm to other prisoners but were done solely for one's own benefit were common; they were judged only from the standpoint of expediency. Such thefts, if committed unselfishly for the good of other prisoners, embodied the highest values, since they served to save the life of one's fellow man.

All the moral norms of the civilized world can, in turn, be reinterpreted in the light of camp conditions and the camp power structure. Camp criteria should be applied to each such norm to determine whether abiding by it would have any relevance for life in Auschwitz, whether it could be put into practice, whether the rules derived from it could be considered at all meaningful in camp conditions.

Such norms were, and once again are, the regulators of life for communities living in civilized, twentieth-century conditions and under social systems appropriate for those conditions. In concentration-camp communities, where prisoners lived in stone-age conditions and under the social system of slavery, these norms were for the most part rendered dysfunctional. The same applied to camp social customs—a slave deprived of his rights had no need for aristocratic manners, nor for the obligatory customs at other social levels.

In normal communities, noble standards abound but are constantly infringed. The smooth conventions of social manners conceal predatory ambitions and egoisms. In camp conditions much asocial behavior must be interpreted as mental disturbance. In that Nazi experimental community whose conditions of life were deliberately demoralizing, the infringement of norms—if such cases did not result in a permanent attitude—should be judged in the context of the force needed to bring them about.

There is no camp prisoner who could responsibly state for certain that, if attacked in the weakest part of his being, he would not have been capable of committing an offense against the most important norms. Those who managed to survive because the camp terror did not strike their weakest point were very fortunate.

And so the judging of prisoner morality is only justified if done in relation to those standards which could be practiced in camp conditions and which were most important in those conditions: they regulated community life so that each person's battle for his own biological survival was not aimed directly against another prisoner and so that advantage could be taken of every opportunity in the battle to save one's fellow prisoners.

Judgment should be further related to the prisoner's place in the camp's structure of violence and to the degree of direct support he had from a group of inmates who acknowledged and practiced basic values. The better a prisoner's situation in the camp and the more closely-knit the informal group in which he could participate, the fewer the moral norms of free men he had to revise. The capacity to act according to the full scope of such norms while at the bottom of the camp structure and without the support of close companions testified to the highest of heroic virtues. In every camp situation there would be prisoners forming into groups—though continually fragmented by the camp system—uniting together in the practice of the basic norm, "Do not harm your neighbor and, if at all possible, save him," even in the most oppressive conditions. It was the prisoner's most important field of battle.

The meaning of this norm was not totally clear-cut. "Harm" and "rescue" denoted endlessly familiar situations. But who was a "neighbor"? How did a person with a chance of saving someone apply that norm to a crowd of neighbors needing to be saved? He could use the principle "whoever is closest to you is your neighbor," or "whoever needs it the most," or "whoever would most effectively benefit from the help you have to offer." In addition to a prisoner's spontaneous reactions in a specific situation, the choice of whom to help was determined by the desire to save the people closest to one, with whom there were bonds of friendship, intellectual and occupational ties.

Every prisoner had his own "neighbors." In the midst of the fight against a world of hatred, as a reaction to a degenerate system of terror, a world of friendship came into being. And precisely in this sense, regardless of prisoner conduct that did not harmonize with the standards of free societies, the concentration camp established a basic norm, the observance of which is everywhere indispensable, and it created a new moral value: that bond with the wronged which demands the greatest renunciations.

Glossary

This glossary is not meant to be all-inclusive.
It is intended as an aid to the reader who may
not be familiar with the terminology that appears
in this book (as well as in many others on the
subject of the Nazi camps) and which was specific
to the concentration camps and the Nazi occupation.
—Trans.

APEL——see ROLL CALL.

"ARBEIT MACHT FREI"——"Work will set you free," sign over main entrance to Auschwitz I.

AUSSENKOMMANDO——A work crew of prisoners laboring in the open air, outside the barbed-wire limits of the camp.

BLOCKÄLTESTE (f.), *BLOCKÄLTESTER* (m.), *BLOCKÄLTESTEN* (pl.)——The barracks supervisor, a male or female prisoner-functionary who was responsible for the inmates of his or her barracks during roll call, for the distribution of food to the prisoners and for order in the barracks.

BLOCKSPERRE——Barracks' closure, prohibition against leaving the barracks.

CANTEEN——A distribution center for tobacco, insect powder, and sometimes other articles.

EFFEKTENKAMMER——Storehouses for the civilian clothes and valuables of non-Jewish prisoners and also for the personal effects of Jewish prisoners and victims; a section of these storehouses was referred to as "Canada."

GESTAPO——Formed in 1933 under Hermann Goering; in 1936 it was combined with the SS under Himmler, who subordinated it to the SD (Security Police), then to the RSHA (Main Security Office) as its 4th Section. The Gestapo was the main organ of coercion in the Third Reich, and together with the SS it implemented policies of terror and extermination in occupied countries.

KAPO——A male or female prisoner-functionary responsible for supervising a work crew.

KOMMANDO——A work crew. There were about 300 work crews at Auschwitz; most contained from 50 to 1200 prisoners, but some were smaller. The smaller ones had a "permanent" staff; that is, the prisoners' numbers were entered in the employment records and noted down by the *Kapo*. Field crews consisted solely of "temporaries."

LAGERÄLTESTE (f.), *LAGERÄLTESTER* (m.), *LAGERÄLTESTEN* (pl.)——A male or female prisoner-functionary responsible for order on the camp premises and in the barracks, the camp boss.

LAGERKAPO——A prisoner-functionary responsible for the total work routine, the chief *Kapo*.

MUSELMANN (sing.), *MUSELMÄNNER* (pl.)——German for "Moslem." In the camps the word carried no religious connotation whatsoever. Used by prisoners and SS alike, it signified a prisoner who showed symptoms of the advanced stages of starvation. Primo Levi explains in his *Survival in Auschwitz* that to become a *Muselmann*, it was "enough to carry out all the orders one receives, to eat only the ration, to observe the discipline of work and the camp routine."

TO ORGANIZE——In the camps the word had several meanings. At its most basic it meant to steal, buy, exchange, or somehow get hold of some article necessary for survival or some luxury item. It also meant to acquire a thing that was needed without wronging another prisoner. Sometimes it meant getting at the storehouses and distributing some articles of daily need to others, without being caught.

POLITISCHE ABTEILUNG——The "political section" of the camp administration. It combined the roles of Gestapo, police, and Ministry of the Interior; it kept records on the prisoners registered in the camp, conducted espionage, prevented escapes, organized the system of punishments and methods of killing. It constituted the principal authority for the apparatus of terror and mass killing in the camp, and although it collaborated closely with the camp commandant, in practice it possessed limitless power over the fates of prisoners.

POSTEN (pl.)——Refers to the SS officers who functioned exclusively as guards, either in the watchtowers that were placed around the camp perimeters, or in the field, watching the work crews. They were also used as additional security for special activities (e.g., "selections," the arrival of a transport).

PRISONER-FUNCTIONARY——Prisoner entrusted with power over others, or with special work in the camp administration.

QUARANTINE CAMP——New inmates were sent to the quarantine camp in Birkenau, Section BIIa (see Figure 2–3) for a period of four to six weeks. This period was a test of physical endurance that only the healthiest survived; it was also a time to learn the camp rules, the language and the songs, and the torments.

REVIER——The camp "hospital." Located in a separate section of the camp, surrounded by barbed wire, it was devoid of medicine, hygiene, and sanitation.

ROLL CALL——Although the term is associated with an ordinary boy scout or army ritual—a simple verification of presence or absence— roll call in the camp served as an additional means of biologically destroying the prisoners by forcing them to endure hours of standing, in their thin rags, unprotected from rain and snow. Roll call occurred before dawn and the forming of work crews and again at dusk after the return from work. Sometimes ordinary roll call lasted as long as four hours. Penal roll calls were inflicted as a collective reprisal for some individual prisoner's misdeed; often they lasted all night long, accompanied by beatings and shootings.

ROUND-UP——Refers to the capturing of civilians at random in Poland. People were picked up on the streets or dragged from their homes and shipped off to forced labor in the Third Reich or in the camps. These round ups became more and more frequent as the war progressed.

SELECTION——Since only those who worked had the right to live, the camp "hospitals" and prisoners' barracks were subject to actions at regular intervals known as "selections." SS doctors carried out selections of disabled prisoners to be sent to the gas chambers. No physical examination took place; the decision of who would live and who would die was made on the basis of a prisoner's outer bearing. Some victims of selection were killed by injections of phenol into the veins or the heart.

S.K.——See *STRAFKOMPANIE.*

SONDERKOMMANDO——The "special work crew," living and working in isolation, utilized in the implementation of assembly-line killing, i.e., gassing of people and burning of bodies.

"SPECIAL TREATMENT" (*SONDERBEHANDLUNG, SB*)——Nazi code name for murder.

SS——Evolved from Hitler's bodyguards (formed in 1923). When

Himmler was placed in command, the SS was subordinate to the SA (a paramilitary organization of the Nazi party, and Hitler's chief weapon in the struggle for power) and was functioning as a security service and the internal police of the party. In 1934 the SS played the principal role in the SA leadership purge and took over the staffing of the concentration camps from the SA. It also became an independent Nazi organization. Himmler gradually extended the power of the SS over the RSHA (Main Security Service) and the Gestapo, and during the war he directed the "nationalities" policy (resettlement, extermination, etc.) of the Third Reich in Nazi-occupied countries. During this time the SS also took over key positions in government, becoming, in the last years of the Reich, the most powerful ruling factor, largely independent of the army (*Wehrmacht*) and the civil service. The Nürnberg Tribunal declared the SS a criminal organization.

STRAFKOMPANIE——The penal crew, known to the prisoners as the "*SK*," lived in separate, locked barracks and performed especially heavy labor; its members were identified by a circular patch sewn on the back of their jackets. Prisoners were assigned to the penal crew for infringing camp regulations, or on the recommendation of the Gestapo, usually for a specified period.

S.V. (SICHERUNGSVERWAHRTE)——A designation for prisoners sent to concentration camps for so-called "preventive detention" after having served prison sentences decreed by Nazi courts.

WINKIEL——Colored triangular patch sewn to the clothes of camp inmates to indicate the category of offense for which they had been imprisoned. See chapter seven, "Colored Triangles."

ZUGANG (sing.), *ZUGÄNGE* (pl.)——A group of newly arrived prisoners before they lost their attributes of "free men and women." It could also mean any newcomer—to camp, to the hospital, to the barracks, etc. New prisoners usually did not understand the conditions into which they had been delivered and for this reason were exposed to especially sadistic bullying.

ZUGANGSBARACKE——The barracks where newcomers to the camp were sent if they arrived at night or if the bathhouse was too crowded. After a while the new prisoners were led to the showers and registered into the camp.

Bibliographical Note

The original Polish edition of *Values and Violence in Auschwitz* (Warsaw: PWN, 1973) contains thirteen pages of bibliography. The reader conversant with Polish is, therefore, directed to this extensive bibliography, drawn entirely from the immense material available in that language on the subject of the camps. For general interest it may suffice to name the most prominent collections of documents and bibliographic material on camp literature in Poland. The following list of sources and locations has been kindly provided by the author for this edition:

Warsaw

Główna Komisja Badania Zbrodni Hitlerowskich w Polsce [Main Commission for the Investigation of Nazi Crimes in Poland]
Biblioteka Narodowa [National Library]
Biblioteka Publiczna Miasta Warszawy [Warsaw Public Library]
Biblioteka Uniwersytecka [University of Warsaw Library]

Kraków

Zeszyty oświęcimskie Przeglądu Lekarskiego [The Auschwitz Notebooks in *Przegląd Lekarski,* the *Medical Review* of the Kraków Medical Association]

Biblioteka Jagiellońska [Jagiellonian University Library]

Oświęcim [Auschwitz]

Muzeum [The Museum]

Other

Various university libraries in the provinces

Index

Acceptance, of force as supreme authority, 18-19, 49, 124

Accuracy, 9, 47

Adamski, Tomasz, 155n

Adaptation to camp life, 100-111, 126-134; ability for, 126; by accepting reduced material needs, 127-128, 138; and categories of powerful authorities, 85; character traits conducive to, 130-131; via collaboration with the structure of terror, 44-50, 126; and economic differences among prisoners, 55; by the intelligentsia, 56-57; by maintaining inner freedom, 127, 128, 132-133; by peasants, 56-57; and philosophical approach to death, 131-132; by previously jailed prisoners, 57-58; by prisoners from the working class, 56-57; psychological mechanisms for, 59-64, 128-134; by resisters to

Nazi occupants, 58; revised values and moral standards for, 138-144; via risk-taking, 63-64, 96, 98, 130; role of psychic shock in, 57-58, 60-61; and social differentiation among prisoners, 55-59, 65-66; socio-economic defense mechanisms for, 100-111; to unsanitary conditions, 46, 60, 128; viewed by Bruno Bettelheim, xxviii, 18, 49, 126, 141; relative to work, 62-64, 129

Aggression: in animal herds, 123; of female prisoner-functionaries, 99, 117; against Poland by Germany, xi; among prisoners, 65-66, 125

Aggressor, identification with, xxviii, 18, 49, 126, 141

Aid: basis for selecting prisoners to receive, 61-62, 144; information transmitted for, 116-117; legends of, 14; for lovers in the same camp,

97; to new prisoners, 61–62; from people outside the camp, xxix, 11–14, 103, 113, 115–116; possibilities for determined by communication, 91; provided by prisoners in stable work crews, 71; to the sick, 73; spontaneous forms of, xxix, 101, 114–118, 119, 129–130, 136. *See also* Cooperation; Defense mechanisms

Alcohol: effect of on SS officials, 64–65, 84–85, 110; as a reward for concentration-camp personnel, 18

Alcoholism, of SS functionaries, 19, 110

American Revolution, xii

Animal herds, behavior of, 123, 125–126

Anonymity of prisoners, 70. *See also* Identity of prisoners

Antagonisms among prisoners, 65–66, 125

Anti-Nazi conspirators, 87

Arrests, based on collective guilt, 86

Arrival time, and survival chances, 58–59

Arts: discussed by prisoners, 119; patronage of by the camp elite, 81–82; Polish, xvii–xviii

Assassins, killing of, 141

Assembly line death industry, 77–80; possessions of victims of, 78, 80, 102–103; reactions of prisoners selected for, 78–79; reactions of prisoners to the threat of, 79–80, 131–132

Atrocities: avoiding naturalistic descriptions of, xxi, 2, 4; knowledge of among future generations, xxv, 2; and optimistic values, xxvii, 4

Attitudes: of concentration-camp survivors, xix, 4; about death, 77, 78–80, 100, 131–132; to make relevant moral choices, 140; among new prisoners, 62; of prisoner-functionaries, 48–50; of self-reliance, 122; of SS functionaries, 18–20. *See also* Values

Auschwitz, xv, 6, 7; administrative divisions of space at, 33–35, 42–43; arrival time of transports to, 58–59; T. Borowski's stories about, xxiii–

xxiv; camp records of, 25, 47, 59–60; 83–84; communication methods among informal groups of prisoners at, 28–43; evaluation of prisoners' moral behavior at, xxi, 138–144; men's camp at, 107, 115; motives for accepting a job at, 18–20; murder methods used at, 54n–55n; as a Nazi "social experiment," 124–127; naturalistic descriptions of horrors of, xxi, 2, 4; number of people exterminated at, 25, 83; organizational structure of with potential for humane relationships, 72, 105, 110–111; organized resistance movement in, 112–122; as a "paradise for green and black badges," 45, 106; registered prisoners at, 25, 59–60; severe climate at, 25–26, 53–54; site and plan of, 24–26; size of national groups of prisoners at, 89–93; social status of SS functionaries at, 20; staff of felons in, 45–50; struggle for power at, 108–109

Auschwitz-Birkenau: protection of women imprisoned at, 117; selection for the gas chamber witnesses by prisoners at, 79; site and plan of, 25, 26–33; subcamps at, 71; women's camp at, 45, 79, 90, 128; Yugoslav female prisoners at, 90–91: work areas in, 35, 37, 40–41

"Auschwitz Group," 117

Auschwitz Museum, xxvii, 24

Auschwitz III—Buna Monowice, 117

Aussenkommando, defined, 145. *See also* Field work crews

Austria, xii, xiii, 91

Austrian prisoners, 91; resistance by, 89

Authority: acceptance of force as a supreme authority, 18–19; of brute force, 9, 49; of prisoner-functionaries, 45–50; resistance toward perverted forms of, xxix, 134; of values vs. power, 133

Authority of terror, 7–10; personality changes resulting from participation in, 20–21, 48–50

Autumn transports, 58–59

Awareness among prisoners: and aggressive behavior to fellow prisoners, 125; of cooperative resistance, 121–122; determinants of, 7; of size of national groups of prisoners, 89–92. *See also* Consciousness

Badges. *See* Colored triangular badges
Baltic countries, xvi
Barbed-wire fences, 26, 34, 79
Barracks: ban against leaving, 35, 145; for the camp elite, 81; congestion in, 46; described, 27–28; for newcomers, 62; for quarantine, 60; transfers from, 34, 46–47
Barracks, supervisors of: duties of, 145; as promoting conflicts among prisoners, 33; "order" inside the camp maintained by, 45–46; as part of the camp power structure, 33, 37, 106; personal relationships between prisoners and, 46–47; role of in the camp market, 102; sexual relationships of, 99
Basic needs, and adaptation to camp life, 127–128, 138, 141
Bathhouse, 37; pranks by staff of, 60; use of, 30, 34
Beatings, 62, 64, 84; avoidance of by hauling sewage, 129; death from, 64; protection from, 119
Behavior: of animal herds, 123, 125–126; different cultural interpretations of, 130; evaluation of prisoners' moral behavior, 138–144; of gas chamber victims, 78–79; of Greek Jews, 91–92, 126; and personality changes, 20–23, 48–50, 84–85, 126–134; of prisoner-functionaries, 48–50; reactions to death and to dying prisoners, 77, 78–80, 131–132; of SS functionaries, 18–22, 70–71, 105, 111; induced by starvation, 74–77, 125
Behaviorist theories, applied to camp life, xxviii
Betrayal, 96
Bettelheim, Bruno: on identification with the aggressor, xxviii, 49, 141n;

The Informed Heart by, xxviin, xxviii, 49n
Biological sciences, and human ethics, xxviii
Birkenau. *See* Auschwitz-Birkenau
Black market, 104. *See also* Camp market
Black triangular badges: Auschwitz as a "paradise" for, 45, 106; dominance of in camp, 88; meaning of, 85, 86; for Gypsies, 92
Blockältesten. See Barracks, supervisors of
Blocksperre, defined, 35, 145
Bodies: as emotionally neutral objects, 131; as raw material for industry, 17, 21, 22, 54n
Bolsheviks, xiii, xiv
Bond, with the wronged, xxx, 144
Bonds among prisoners: as basis for giving aid, 61; of friendship, 34, 96, 144; humanist values as, 3, 6, 11–14, 59, 121–122, 133–134, 139–141; between loved ones, 96–97; of nationality, 107; established by "old numbers," 92; established by similar experiences and common goals, 30, 33, 52, 92
Borowski, Tadeusz: quoted from *World of Stone*, 68; short stories about Auschwitz by, xxiii–xxiv
Bowl, ownership of, 128
Bread, 128
Bribes: accepted by prisoner-functionaries, 46, 48, 102, 109; and the camp elite, 82; via food, 103–104; people susceptible to, 109; use of victims' property for, 80, 102–103, 104–105
Brutality: in the exercise of authority, 45, 46, 49, 124; among prisoners, 65; toward Poles, xvi; toward the dying, 132
Bullock, Alan, 7n, 8n
Bunks: acquisition of, 62; as location for consolidating groups of prisoners, 33–34, 40, 42. *See also* Sleeping places
Burlesque theaters, xvii
Business relations: among the camp

elite, 82; between prisoners and SS officials, 105, 110
Byelorussia, xvi

Camp "diet," adaptation to, 128. See also Food rations
Camp gate, 102; German motto on, 116-117; passage through by work crews, 40-41
Camp hospital. See Hospital
Camp life: crucial role of food packages in, 103-104; death from starvation in, 76-77; detachment from via imagination, 132-133; eroticism in, 97-99; functions of various prisoners in, 37, 106, 108, 118; initiation into, 59-63; laws of, 130; leisure activities in, 81-82, 118-119; literature about, xxiii-xxv, xxvi-xxviii, 97, 125; love in, 35, 94-99; as ordinary life, 126: prisoners' warning signals in, 84-85; revised moral standards in, 137-144; routine of, 68; threat of death as part of, 74-80, 131; understanding the reality of, xxiv, 2, 4, 77. See also Adaptation to camp life; Camp power structure; Survival chances
Camp market: fluctuating prices in, 104; food packages in, 103-104; function and evolution of, xxi, 101-105; possessions of murdered victims in, 102-103, 104-105; social barriers breached by, 103-105; survival via, 109
Camp power structure, 37; battle for status in, 106-111; different stages in the history of, 108; dominance in by national groups of prisoners, 66, 108; elite in, 80-82; groups of prisoners gradually taking control of, 107-109; vs. hierarchy of values among prisoners, 133-134; influence of prisoners over SS officials, 70-72, 109-111; overcoming social barriers in, 70-72, 103-105; participation in the resistance movement evaluated in terms of, 120-122; predominance of various colored badges relative to, 88, 107, 108; prisoner morality evaluated in terms of, 66-67, 143-144;

prisoners as the bottom of, 74, 76, 77, 144; rescue strategy of reserving places in, 107; role of specialized functions in, 106, 108, 118; role of the camp market in, 104-105, 109; size of groups dependent on status in, 89-92; status of prisoner-functionaries in, 48-50
Camp regulations: blame for infractions of, 142; decision to disobey, 130; enforcement of, 45; opportunities to break, 71; and penal crew, 69; punishments for breaking, 40, 41, 69
Camus, Albert: chapter epigraphs by, xxvi; on humanists, xxiii, 1; quotations from The Plague, 1, 24, 51, 83, 94
"Canada", 145
Canteen, 37; coupons for, 102; described, 145
Career occupations: of SS functionaries, 18-22; and survival in concentration camps, 55-57
Carpenters, 72
Catholic Church, xiii, xxiv; and reviews of Values and Violence, xxiv
Chamberlain, Neville, xv-xvi
Chapin, Francis S., 124n
Children: badges worn by, 86-87; kidnapping of, xviii
Christianity: norms of revised for camp conditions, 139, 141-142, 144; values of among Polish prisoners, 136
Cigarettes, 101; as unit of payment, 104
City-states, compared to subcamps, 30, 33-35, 42
Civilized norms vs. revised values in camp, 125-126, 138-143
Class antagonisms among prisoners, 65-66
Class Structure in the Social Consciousness (S. Ossowski), xx
Clergymen, 56; death of, xviii, 16
Climate, at Auschwitz, 25-26, 53-54
Clothing, 46, 47; depositories for, 37; inadequate, 53-54, 128; for the camp elite, 81; in the camp market,

102, 103; colored triangular badges on, 85–89; conflicts over distribution of, 66; penalties for having more than regulation attire, 69; and prostitution, 99; unsanitary condition of, 60; worn by female prisoner-functionaries, 109

"Code of chivalry," 123

Cognitive disturbances, 20. *See also* Mental disturbances

Collaboration: absent in Poland, 11, 136; forms of adaptation based on, 126; by prisoner-functionaries, 44–50. *See also* Aggressor, identification with

Collective defense mechanisms: via the camp market, 101–105; to sustain mental endurance, 119–120; warning signals as, 84–85. *See also* Defense mechanisms; Resistance

Colored triangular badges, 85–89; Auschwitz as a "paradise" for green and black, 45, 106; erroneous identification by, 86–87, 91; green, 107, 111; for Gypsies, 92; predominance of in camp life, 88, 107, 108; red, 90, 106; yellow, 86, 91

Commonwealth of Poland and Lithuania, xii, xiv

Communication among prisoners, 34–35, 40; bunks and "roosts" as location for, 33–34, 40, 42, 117; distorted by oral messages, 42–43; as essential for receiving help, 91; between "old timers" and adapted prisoners, 118; linguistic barriers to, 65, 117, 130; via the resistance movement, 114, 115–116, 118, 119; via tattoed numbers, 92; work sites as a location for, 37, 40, 42, 63. *See also* Warnings among prisoners

Community of prisoners: attitudes toward victims of torture, 126–127; character traits to gain support from, 130–131; conflicts in, 65–66, 125; cultural environment of, 128; elite in, 80–82; homogeneity in, 33, 52; identification by colored triangular badges, 85–92; identification by letters and numbers, 25n, 89–90, 92;

initiation into, 59–61; love and eroticism in, 94–99; literary interests among, 118–119; methods to abolish solidarity in, 44–50; mutual aid and cooperation in, 61–63, 117–118, 130–131; Nazi authority viewed by, 59, 133–134, 136–137; recipients of food packages as a privileged group in, 103–104; revised hierarchy of values in, 137–144; specialized job functions in, 106–107, 118; terror of the stronger over the weaker in, 66; values as a unifying bond in, 3, 6, 11–14, 59, 121–122, 133–134, 139–144. *See also* Bonds among prisoners; Groups of prisoners

Concentration camps: administrative divisions of space in, 33–35, 42–43; arrival time to, 58–59; compared to city-states, 30, 33–35, 42; different periods in the history of, 108; influence of outside world on, 6–14, 109, 113, 114, 115; information about transmitted to non-Nazi countries, 115; as institutions of state crime, 15–23; literature about, xxiii–xxviii, 97, 125; new value created by, xxx, 144; "order" in, 45–46; prisoners' perceptions of space and dwellings in, 41–42; sexual distinctions in social structure of, 53, 98; as a social experiment, 123–127; sociological approach to, xxi, 6; social differentiation relative to survival in, 51–59; understanding the reality and horrors of, xxiv, xxi, xxvii, 2, 4, 77; unsanitary conditions in, 30, 46, 60, 128. *See also* Adaptation to camp life; Camp power structure; Death; Terror

Concentration-camp personnel: competition and rivalry among, 21–23; duties of, 15–18; moral degeneracy of, 20–21; motivational patterns and attitudes of, 18–19; punishable deeds of, 21–22; relationships with prisoner-functionaries, 50; rewards of, 18, 21; selection and recruitment of, 19–20; theft of prisoners' possessions by, 19, 21–22. *See also* SS officials

Concentration-camp prisoners: aggressive behavior among, 65–66, 125; callousness of, 131–132; communication among, 34–35, 40, 42–43, 91, 114, 115–116, 118, 119; economic differences among, 55; educational levels of, 56–57; elite among, 80–82; evaluation of behavior of, 138–144; German criminals as, 57; mental endurance of, 119–120; Nazi "ideological" categories of, 25n, 54–55, 85–92; physical appearance of, 60, 61, 65–66, 70; in positions of authority, 44–50; size of national groups perceived by, 89–93; social differentiation among, 51–59, 65–66, 135; symbols denoting categories of, 85–93; as test material for pseudomedical experiments, 16–17, 22, 73. *See also* Bonds among prisoners; Community of prisoners; Groups of prisoners

Conflicts among prisoners: ability to alleviate, 130; causes of, 65–66

"Conscience," identified with obedience to power, 49

Consciousness: centered on loved ones, 94–97; changed by participating in the mechanism of killing, 49–50; determined by existence, xxi, 137, 141; of the living space, 41–42; of the size of national groups of prisoners, 89–92

Conspiratorial organizations, 112–122; goal of, 113; and identification via triangular badges, 87. *See also* Resistance movement

Cooperation: capacity for, 101, 120, 130–131; in the camp market, 101–105; for survival, 61–63, 117–118; between Russian and Polish prisoners, 90; between SS officials and prisoner-functionaries, 48–50

Corpse. *See* Bodies

"Courts," of the camp elite, 81–82

Crematories, 31; capacity of, 30; destruction of, 115; for industrial genocide, 79; observing the smoke from, 93, 132; use of 54n

Crime, state institutions of, 15–23

Crimea, xvi

Criminal activities, Nazi: attempts to obliterate traces of, 10, 18, 78, 83; and demise of humanist values, 7–10; hierarchical levels of, 22–23; moral price for, 50; motivations for, 18–21, 48–50; recognized by Nazi officials as criminal, 10, 23, 83; responsibility for, 22, 85; training for, 9, 20, 124; viewed by prisoners, 59, 133–134, 136–137

Criminal gang, 78, 133; power struggles and conflicts within, 22–23; role of in the development of Nazism, 7–10

Criminal prisoners: in camp hospitals, 72; as demoralized and degenerated, 45, 47, 49–50; in middle levels of power, 108; motivations of, 48–50; in positions of authority, 45–50; survival chances of, 57. *See also* Prisoner-functionaries

Cultural barriers, 126

Cultural tastes, of the camp elite, 81–82

Culture, Polish, xvii–xviii

Cyprian, Tadeusz, 21n

Czarnkowski, Stefan, 8n

Czechoslovakia, xvi

Dancers, 81

Danger, reactions to, 129–130

Danzig, xv

Dawidowicz, Lucy S., x

Death: as an assembly line industry, 77–80; attitudes toward, 77, 78–80, 100, 131–132; caused by starvation, 74–77; as an escape, 131; false reports on causes of, 17; indicated by "special treatment" symbol, 60; insensitivity resulting from daily contact with, 77, 131–132; mental submission to, 100; as objective of concentration camps, 15–17, 44, 46, 47, 54–55, 74–80, 100, 115n; peaceful, 72; power to dispense, 19; social engineering for, 124; witnessing of, 77, 125, 131; worst kind of 76

Decalogue, 139, 141–142

Decembrists, xiii

Defense mechanisms: collective, 101-105, 119-120; and initiation into camp life, 60-61; lies as, 142; necessity for, 114; and reactions to dead and dying prisoners, 77, 78-80, 131-132; socio-economic, 100-111; and unequal chances of survival, 59-67. *See also* Self-defense mechanisms

Defensive adaptation: methods of inner resistance for, 127-134; strategy for, 126, 128

"Delousing" operations, 30, 35

Demographic policy, Nazi, xviii

Deportations, xv, xvi, xviii

Des Pres, Terrence: camp survival behavior evaluated by, xxvii-xxix; *The Survivor*, xxvii; theory of biological base of ethics conceived by, xxviii

Desensitization, 131-132

Diseases, 60n; contagious, 72; and starvation, 74-77

Disinfection, 37. *See also* "Delousing" operations

Doctors, camp prisoners as, 56, 73

Doctors, German: lack of medical ethics, 73; selection of prisoners for death, 78, 147

Documents: camp records, 25n; preserved by the *Sonderkommando*, 78; transmitted by the resistance movement, 115

Dominance, in camp structure, 66, 108. *See also* Camp power structure

Dreams, 132-133

Dubos, René, 123

Dutch Jews, 79n

Dying: reactions to, 77, 78-80, 100, 132; sequence for, 16, 54

Dziubińska, Barbara, 112n

E, significance of, 25n, 89

Eastern European countries: Marxism in, xix; Nazi plans for, xvi-xvii, xviii

Economic differences, and survival of prisoners, 55-56

Education: and capacity for endurance, 57; and knowledge of concentration camp horrors, xxv, 2; in occupied Poland, xiv, xvii; and survival chances among prisoners, 55-56

Effektenkammer, 70; described, 145

Elderly, 53; death of, 54n

Electricians, 70

Elite prisoners, 80-82

Emotional needs: awakening of, 97; fulfilled via homosexual relationships, 98

Emotions, of prisoners with loved ones, 94-97

Emperor of the Earth (C. Miłosz), xxx

Endurance: capacity for, 57; collective defense mechanisms for, 119-120; and mental disturbances, 125, 127; signified by "old number," 58; impact of torture on, 126-127

Engineers, 56

Enlightenment, ideas of, xii

Epidemics, 60n

Equality, socialist ideal of, 6, 139, 141

Eroticism, 97-99; bisexual, 99; dependent on status in camp structure, 65, 98, 142; homosexual, 98-99

Escape: via death, 131; hope for, 52; plans for, 115

Ethical standards: biological basis of, xxviii-xxix; of doctors, 73; situational, xxiv-xxv, 137-144; abolished by starvation, 75-76

Europe: contemporary attitudes in about concentration camps, 3-4; 1848 revolutions, xiii

European culture, values of, 6-7, 11-12, 14, 20, 53, 59, 122, 139-144. *See also* Humanist values

Evaluation: of participation in the resistance movement, 120-122; of prisoners' moral behavior, xxvii-xxix, 138-144

Evil, xxvi; concentration camps as, 4; fight against, xvi; recognition of, 2; refusal to rationalize the problems of, xxx; suffering caused by, xxiii

Exhaustion, 97, 98; from overwork, 117n

"Existence determines consciousness," xxi, 137, 141

Extermination, 52; as goal of camp officials, 100; guilt for, 22-23, 85; Nazi criteria for ranking victims selected for, 16, 25n, 54-55; of the physically weak, 53, 54n, 78; records of, 17, 54n, 83; secrecy of, 17-18, 78, 83, 115

Familial groups, in "roosts," 33-34, 40, 42, 117
Family, prisoners' concern for, 94-96
Farm crops, 102
Fate, 132
Fear, 137; alleviated by humor, 129; control of, 130; of physical and mental torture, 13, 50
Fejkiel, Wladyslaw, 73n; quoted on the effects of starvation, 75, 76
Felons: as prisoner-functionaries, 45-49; and triangular badges worn by, 87. See also Criminal prisoners
Female prisoners. See Women
Field work crews (Aussenkommandos): communication methods of, 40, 42-43; compared to stable work crews, 70; farm crops acquired by, 102; informal groups among, 37, 40-41; length of time spent in the same, 64-65; privileges of supervisors of, 47-48. See also Work crews
Flossenbürg, Germany (concentration camp), xix
Food, 128; conflicts among prisoners during distribution of, 66; opportunities to obtain extra, 70; and prostitution, 99; and self-defense, 128; stolen by starving prisoners, 75-76; taking risks to obtain, 63-64, 96
Food packages: crucial role of in camp life, 103-104; for Jews, 103; privilege of receiving, 98, 103
Food rations: amount of, 28, 30, 76; appropriated by prisoner-functionaries, 46, 47-48; in the camp market, 101-102; decline in theft of, 104; and inner resistance, 128
Foreign languages, knowledge of, 56, 65, 117

Fortunetellers, 82
Frankl, V. E., 59n
Freedom, inner: imagination as an ally of, 132-133; as a self-defense mechanism, 127-128, 141
French Revolution, xii
Friendship: bonds of, 34, 96, 144; Nazi reprisals for acts of, 14
Future plans, 119

Gamble for life, 132
Games, as defense mechanisms, 129
"Gang" concept, applied to Nazi officials, 8, 9-10, 22-23, 78, 133
Gansters, Nazi: stereotype of, 10, 136; social experiment conducted by, 123-127. See also Criminal activities, Nazi
Gas chambers: and breaking the ban against leaving the barracks, 35; capacity of, 54n; possessions of victims of, 102-103; selection for, 35, 54n, 73-74, 78, 129, 147; technology for, 78; witnesses of, 79, 93. See also Victims' possessions
Generalplan Ost, xvi
Genocide: and concept of criminal gang, 10, 78; industrial, 77-80; and international law, 7; motives and rationalizations for, 18-19; obliteration of the traces of, 18, 78, 83; performed as work, 21
German doctors: medical ethics of, 73; selection of prisoners for death, 73-74, 78, 147
German language, knowledge of, 56, 64
German nationality, conceived as superior, 9, 17n, 22, 56
German prisoners, 55; as criminals, 57, 64; number of at Auschwitz, 89; prostitutes among, 65
German prostitutes, 65, 106, 129
German shepherds, 41, 85
German society, acceptance of Nazism in, 7-10, 124
Germanization, xv, xvi, xviii
Germany, xiii, xv, xvi, xviii, xix, xxix, 7-10, 91, 106, 122, 136. See also Third Reich; Nazi government

Gestapo: brutality of, 13; evolution and functions of, 146; imprisonment by, 55; interrogation by, 87; as jailers, 58; Szucha and Pawiak prisons of, 13n; torture by, xviii

Glasses, wearing of, 56

Główna Komisja Badania Zbrodni Hitlerowskich w Polsce (Poland's War Crimes Investigation Commission), xxiii, 3n, 15n, 25n, 53n, 149

Glinska, A., 138n

Gold teeth, use of, 17n, 54n

Government General, in Poland, xv, xvii

Greece, 91

Greed of SS officials, 19, 71, 105, 109-110

Greek Jews: behavior of, 91-92; death of, 74, 92; inability to adapt to camp life, 126; problems of communication with, 91

Greek prisoners, survival chances of, 54

Green triangular badges: Auschwitz as a "paradise" for, 45, 106; behavior of prisoners with, 111; confused meaning of, 87; power of prisoners with, 107, 111; significance of, 85-89 passim

Groups of prisoners, xxi; bunks and barracks as basis for, 33-34, 40, 62, 117; centers of camp power gradually controlled by, 107; character traits needed to gain support from, 130-131; composed of inmates from the same prison, 58; demarcated by letters and numbers, 89-93; designated by colored triangular badges, 85-89; formed by Russian prisoners, 90; formed by prisoners from the same transport, 62, 114; influence over SS officials acquired by, 71-72; Jehovah's Witnesses among, 86, 88-89; judgment of prisoner morality relevant to, 143-144; "leisure activities" among, 118-119: method to abolish cohesiveness of, 44-50; within the resistance movement, 114; in stable work crews, 71-72; values of, 101; work sites as basis

for, 37, 40, 117. See also Solidarity among prisoners

Grzesiuk S., 126n

Guards (Posten): acts of terrorism by, 48; effect of alcohol on, 64-65; authority exercised by, 85; functions of, 146-147; at the work site, 41

Guilt: caused by conflict between conduct and values, 139; from psychological collapse induced by torture, 126-127; rationalizations to reduce, 49; of SS officers, 85

Gumkowski, Janusz, xvin, xviin

Gypsies: camp for, 71, 92; death of, 16, 71n, 92; mass murder of, 54; registered at Auschwitz, 25; symbols for identification of, 25n, 92

Hair: of female prisoners, 60, 91; use of, 17n, 54n

Herds of animals. See Animal herds, behavior of

Heroism, and values, 141, 144

Himmler, Heinrich, xvii

Hitler, Adolf: defeat of, 126; demographic policy of, xviii; on plan to kill Poles, xvi; social experiment of, 127; storm troopers of, 7-8

Hoess, Rudolf, 7n, 8n, 15n

"Holocaust literature," xxvii

Hołuj, Tadeusz, 21n, 112n

Home, for camp prisoners, 33, 42

Home Army, Polish, xiv, 79n, 114

Homogeneity among prisoners, 33, 52

Homosexuality, 98, 99

Hope: and adaptation to camp life, 59; existence of, 52, 122; information transmitted to sustain, 42-43, 119; irrational, xxix, 52, 100; to shatter the terror, 14; for survival, 52, 62

Horrors. See Atrocities

Hospital (Revier): ambiguous privilege of staying at, 64, 72-74; death in, 64, 72, 76; delivery of medicines and extra food to, 73, 116; described, 28, 147; and selection of sick prisoners for death, 73-74, 78, 147

Hostages, 58, 87

Hostility, of Poles toward Germans, 11

"Human" vs. "non-human" beings, 8; in Nazi ideology, 20-21, 111; overcoming the barriers of, 72, 111; Slavs as subhuman, xviii

Human nature, as viewed by camp survivors, 4

Humanism, interpreted by Anna Pawełczyńska, xxix-xxx

Humanist values: battle for among camp prisoners, 3, 6, 11-14, 59, 101, 121-122, 133-134, 137, 139-141, 144; belief in the triumph of, 14, 133-134; as common attribute among prisoners, 59, 122, 133, 139-140; diminished in Nazi Germany, 8-9; effect of on prisoners' attitudes and behavior, 6-7, 11-14; expressed by SS officers, 111; linked with the Polish national struggle, 11-14, 136-137; support groups for in German society, 9

Humanists, prevention of evil and suffering by, xxiii, 1

Humor: accepting reduced material needs with, 127, 128; caused by social differentiation among prisoners, 65, 66; in confronting death, 132; efforts to create, 61; as mechanism of collective defense, 119-120; as method of inner resistance, 126, 129, 130, 132

Hungary, 91

Hunger, tolerance of, 128

Hygiene. See Unsanitary conditions

Identification with the aggressor, xxviii, 18, 49, 126, 141

Identity of prisoners: individual names for, 55n, 59-60, 87; via letters and numbers, 25n, 89-92; and pre-camp roles, 71, 119; via serial numbers, 60, 87, 92; via triangular badges on jackets, 85-89

Imagination, and inner freedom, 132-134

Industrial death, 77-80

Industrial tycoons, 22

Inequality of survival chances, 61-67

Informal groups. See Groups of prisoners

Information: circulated among prisoners, 35, 42-43, 79, 84-85; transmitted via the resistance movement, 114, 115-116, 118, 119

Informed Heart, The. See Bettelheim, Bruno

Injections, death from, 17n, 55n, 147

Inner freedom: sustaining of, 127, 128, 132-133; victory achieved by, 141

Inner resistance, 2, 128-134. See also Self defense mechanisms

Insects, 128

Institute of Hygiene, 70n

Institutions: of mass murder, 77-80; of state crime, 15-23

Instrumental values, 9

Intelligence: and level of endurance, 57n; to make relevant moral choices, 140

Intelligentsia, 16; as go-betweens in communication among prisoners, 65, 117; gradual seizure of power by, 107; elimination of Polish, xvi, xvii, xviii; in the resistance movement, 117; shot by German army squads, xv; survival chances of as camp prisoners, 56-57

International law, 7, 10

International Tribunal, xvin, 2-3, 21, 148

Interrogation, xviii, 57n, 87

Irrational hope, xxix, 52, 100

Isolation, 6, 11; of penal crew prisoners, 69; of the Sonderkommando, 79; of subcamps, 71

Iwaszko, Tadeusz, 115n

Jagoda, Z., 60n

Jailed prisoners: adaptation to camp life by, 57-58; hope for rescue by, 52

Jehovah's Witnesses: resistance to Nazism by, 88-89; triangular badges to identify, 86, 88

Jewish Greek prisoners, adaptation to camp life by, 74, 91-92, 126

Jews, xv, xviii, 16; colored triangular

badges on jackets of, 86, 91; mass murder of, 54, 78; registered at Auschwitz, 25; tattooed numbers for, 92

Joys, and defensive adaptation to camp life, 126, 129

Judgment: of participating in the resistance movement, 120–122; of morality relative to the camp reality, 138–144

Kamiński, Andrzej Józef, 7n, 8n
Kapo, 106; functions of, 47, 146. See also Prisoner-functionaries
Kąkol, Kazimierz, 2n
Kelar, Wiesław, 97n
Kępiński, Antoni, 4, 77n
Killing, 49; and revised norms, 141–142. See also Death
Kitchens, 37, crew for, 102
Kłodziński, Stanisław, 54n, 60n, 115n
Kobielski, Franciszek, 112n
Kommando, 146. See also Work crews
Kraków, Poland. xv, 25, 92
Kret, J., 56n

Labor, by concentration-camp prisoners, 16–17, 35–42. See also Slave labor; Work crews
Laboratory experiments, 70n
Lagerältesten, responsibilities of, 45–46, 146
Lagerkapo, duties of, 47, 146
Landscaping crews, 70
Languages, knowledge of, 56, 65, 117
Laughter, 61, 119–120. See also Humor
Laundries, 37
Leach, Catherine S., introduction by, xi–xxxi
Legends: of attempts to give aid; of great love within the camp, 97
Leisure activities: of the camp elite, 81–82; among prisoners, 118–119
Leszczyński, Kazimierz, xvin, xviin
Letters, to indicate nationality of prisoners, 25n, 89, 92
Libraries, Nazi plundering of, xviii
Lies, revised moral standards for, 142
Linguistic barriers, 56, 65, 117, 130; of Greek Jewish prisoners, 91, 126;

role of in the camp power structure, 107
Literature: about concentration camps, xxiii–xxviii, 97, 125; discussed by prisoners, 119
Lithuania, xii, xiii–xiv
Living space, 24–43; confinement and congestion in, 46, 123, 124; the "meadow" in, 34–35; mud in, 28, 42; as perceived by the prisoners, 41–42; required by Germany, xvi; as a term, xxiv. See also Barracks; Work sites
Looting. See Theft
Love: camp legends of, 97; Christian norms for, 139, 141, 144
Loved ones: communication among, 35, 96, 97; concern for, 94–96; interrupted first love, 96–97; in the same camp, 35, 96, 97, 98; as a source of strength, 96, 97, 123, 133
Loyalty, manifestations of, 120, 122
Lublin, xv, 92
Luck, 62, 67, 126
Łukowski, Jerzy, 112n
Lwów, Poland, xv

Majdanek, women's camp in, 45, 108
Male work crews, 99
Marriages of convenience, 98
Marxism: appeal of in Poland, xix; vs. Catholicism, xxx; interpretation of camp experience via, xxiv; as viewed by S. Ossowski, xx; viewed by A. Pawełczyńska, xx–xxi
Marxist reviews, of Values and Violence, xxiv–xxv
Masłowski, J., 60n
Mass executions: collective guilt as base for, xvi; of Poles, xvi, xviii
Mass murder: as an industrialized institution, 77–80; of Jews, 54, 78. See also Death
Material needs, reduced, 127–128, 138, 141
"Meadow," role of, 34–35
Medical experiments, 70n. See also Pseudomedical experiments
Medicines: delivery of, 116, 118; obtaining of, 71, 73

Mental disturbances: asocial behavior from, 143; causes of, 125, 127
Mental endurance: efforts to sustain, 119–120; to maintain inner freedom, 127
Messages, distorted, 42–43
Miłosz, Czesław, xxx–xxxi
Molotov-Ribbentrop Pact, xv
Money, desired by SS officers, 105
Moral choices, capacity to make relevant, 140
Moral conviction, as basis of resistance movements, xv–xvi, 136
Moral degeneracy, 20–21, 49
Moral standards: capacity for creativity with, 140; created by the concentration camps, xxx, 144; judging of, 138–144; Nazi transformation of, 8–10, 20; revised for camp conditions, 137–143. *See also* Humanist values; Norms; Values
Motivational patterns: of paid concentration-camp personnel, 18–19; of prisoner-functionaries, 48–50; of prisoners with specialized camp functions, 106
Motto: on camp gate at Auschwitz, 116–117, 145; of resistance at Auschwitz, 127, 129
Murder: assembly-line techniques for, 54, 77–80; to enforce camp regulations, 45; methods for, 16–17, 54n–55n, 77–80; Nazi code name for, 148; of prisoners in work crews, 47. *See also* Death
Muselmänner, xxi; at bottom of camp structure, 74, 76, 77; death of, 76; described, 146; ethical standards of, 66, 75–76; Greek Jewish women as, 126; psychological changes in, 74–77, 97. *See also* Starvation

Names of prisoners: in camp records, 59–60; unknown, 87; for prisoners shot to death, 55n. *See also* Identity of prisoners
Napoleon, xiii
National barriers, overcome by the resistance movement, 117

National identity, Polish, xiii, xvii–xviii
National mobilization, in occupied Poland, xiv, 11–14
Nationaltiy: and administrative divisions in camps, 33; as basis for a place in the camp power structure, 89–92, 107–108; as cause of conflicts among prisoners, 65–66; German attitudes of superiority, 9, 17, 56; indicated by letters, 25n, 89, 92; and opportunities to make contacts outside the camps, 114; role of in Polish resistance, 11, 136; size of national groups of prisoners, 89–92; and survival chances, 16, 54–55, 91–92
Nazi government: directives for mass murder by, 17, 21, 78; evolution of, 7–10; and German opposition groups, 9; living to see the end of, 52, 132; responsibility for crimes by, 22–23; social engineering applied by, 124–127, 136; social experiment conducted by, 123–127; status in, 9–10; systematic destruction of Poles and Polish culture by, xvi–xviii; viewed by concentration-camp prisoners, 59, 133–134, 136–137. *See also* Criminal activities, Nazi; SS officials
Needs, reduction of, 127–128, 138, 141
Neighboring bunks. *See* Bunks
Neighbors, Christian vs. camp norms for, 139–142, 144
Newcomers (*Zugänge*): arrival time of, 58–59; attitudes of, 62; bath of, 30; defined, 148; helped by adapted prisoners, 61–62; shock experienced by, 57–58, 60; Yugoslav female prisoners among, 91
Norms: and development of Nazi criminal activities, 8; civilized compared to values revised for camp life, 125–126, 138–144; eliminated as dysfunctional in camp conditions, 139, 141–144; generated by concentration camps, xxx, 144; and meaning of "neighbor," 144; and weakness, 140, 143. *See also* Moral standards

Numbers identifying prisoners, 60, 87, 92

Nürnberg International Military Tribunal, xvi*n*, 2-3, 21, 148

Obedience: to camp regulations, 130; as an instrumental value in German society, 9; moral significance of, 136; to Nazi authority, 9, 10, 49; social engineering methods to produce, xvii, 124

Objectivity, of A. Pawełczyńska, xx, 1-2

Occupational contacts, among work crews, 40

Occupational ties, 144

Occupations. *See* Career occupations

Occupied countries, xv-xvi, 10, 112. *See also* Poland, Nazi occupation of

October Revolution of 1917, xiii

"Old number," significance of, 58, 92

"Old timers," communication among, 118

Oral messages, 166; distorted, 42-43

"Order" in camp, 45-46

"Organize:" for survival needs, 62, 63, 65; meaning of, 146

Ossowski, Stanisław: award named after, xxiii; influence on Anna Pawełczyńska, xx-xxi

Ostankiewicz, Czesław, 112n

Outside world: contacted by the resistance movement, 109, 113, 114, 115; values of as a frame of reference for resistance, 6-7, 11-14, 133-134, 136-137, 138-144. *See also* Humanist values

Package depot, 37, 70; ingenuity of prisoners working at, 103

Palarczykowa, Anna, 84n, 86n

Paris Commune, xiii

Patriotism, role of in Polish resistance to Nazi terror, xv, xvi-xvii, 11-12, 136

Pawełczyńska, Anna, 1-5: academic career of, xix-xxiii; arrest and imprisonment of, xviii; birth of, xi; doctoral dissertation by, xxii; epigraphs at chapter heads by, xxvi, 15, 44, 135; literary style of, xxiv-xxvi; as member of the Resistance, xiv, xviii-xix; moral judgments on Nazism by, xxix, 3-4; objectivity of, xx, 1-2; personal humanism of, xxix-xxx; political and sociological perspectives of, xx-xxi; value systems analyzed by, xxiv-xxv, xxix-xxx, 137-144

Pawiak prison, xviii, 13

Peasants: relationships with intelligentsia in camp, 65-66; survival chances of, 56-57

Penal crew (*Strafkompanie*): living and working conditions of, 64, 69, 148; survival chances of, 69

Penal roll calls, 129-130

Perceptions. *See* Consciousness

Personality: role of in adaptation and survival, 57, 59, 126, 131-133

Personality changes: and emotional callousness toward death, 126, 131-133; from participating in an authority of terror, 20-21, 48-50; of prisoners with loved ones, 95-97

Phenol injections, death from, 17n, 55n, 147

Physical weakness. *See* Weak prisoners

Piłsudski, Józef, xiv

Poetry, 119

Poland: appeal of Marxism in, xix; attitudes toward Germans in, 3, 11; battles for independence of, xiii-xiv, 11, 114, 136; German invasion of, xiv-xv, 10-11; Home Army in, xiv, 79n, 114; national struggle in linked with humanist values, 11-14, 136-137; partitions of, xi, xii-xiii, xv, 11, 136; rebellions of 1830 and 1863 in, xiii; social reform in, xii; traditions of patriotism and Christianity in, xv, xvi-xvii, 11-12, 136

Poland, Nazi occupation of, xiv-xviii: attempts to destroy Polish art and culture, xvii-xviii; humanist and patriotic values as base for resistance, xv, xvi-xvii, 11-14, 135; mass executions of Poles during, xv, xvi,

xviii, 54; national mobilization during, xiv, 11–12; number of Poles killed during, xviii
Poliakov, Leon, 70n
Polish Academy of Sciences, xxi, xxii, xxiii
Polish prisoners: actively involved in the resistance, 12, 90, 113–114; cooperation with Russian prisoners, 90; help for Jewish, 91; patriotic and religious values as base for resistance by, 11–14, 135
Polish Resistance, xiv, xv, xviii–xix, 11, 12, 90, 113–114
Polish Sociological Association, xxiii
Polish Underground. *See* Polish Resistance
Political information, transmission of, 119
Political prisoners: in camp hospitals, 73; gradual seizure of power by, 107, 108; in the resistance movement, 90, 115; torture and rescue of, 13; triangular badges on jackets of, 85–88 *passim*, 90, 106
Politicians, use of camp lessons by, xx–xxi, xxv, 2
Politische Abteilung, 107, 146
Pornography, xvii
Posten. See Guards
Potato storehouse, 37, 70
Power, equated with self-worth, 49
Power structure. *See* Camp power structure
Prisoner(s). *See* Concentration-camp prisoners
Prisoner-administrators, functions of, 45–48. *See also* Prisoner-functionaries
Prisoner-functionaries, 44–50; abuses of authority by, 46; advances into the power structure by, 50, 107; authority and duties of, 45–50; bribed by prisoners, 103–104, 109; brutality of female, 117; to diminish prisoner solidarity, 44–50; defined, 147; educated prisoners hated by, 56; as degenerated and demoralized, 45, 47, 49–50; guard duties of, 34; as helpful to other prisoners, 50, 106–107; and love between male

and female prisoners, 97; motivations of, 48–50, 109; personal relationships with prisoners, 46–47, 48, 50, 70, 72, 106–107; privileges of, 46, 47–48, 49; sexual needs of, 98, 99; as supervisors of work crews, 40, 41, 45, 47–48; use of terror by, 40; use of washrooms by, 30; women as, 109, 117
Prisons: recognition of prisoners from the same, 92; torture in and rescue from, 12–14
Privileges: of avoiding beatings while hauling sewage, 129; of the camp elite, 80–82; of participating in the resistance movement, 120–121; of prisoner-functionaries, 46, 47–48, 49; of receiving food packages, 98, 103–104; of working in stable work crews, 64, 69–72
Privileges, ambiguous: of prisoner's name in the camp records, 59–60; of admittance into the camp hospital, 64, 72–74
Prostitutes: German, 65, 106, 129; payment to, 99; role of in camp, 65
Prussia, xii
Psychological mechanisms for adaptation, 59–64, 128–134. *See also* Adaptation to camp life
Pseudomedical experiments: barracks for, 26; prisoners as test material for, 16–17, 22; to test sterilization methods, 55n
Psychic shock, and adaptation to camp life, 57–58, 60
Psychoanalysis, applied to behavior in camps, xxviii, xxix
Psychological changes, from starvation, 74–77. *See also* Personality changes
Public Opinion Research Center, in Poland, xxi–xxii
Punishments: for prisoners who break camp regulations, 17, 40, 41, 46, 69; for SS functionaries, 21–22

Quarantine: barracks for, 60n; camp for, 147; small groups formed during, 62

Quick reflexes, 130; and survival chances, 62, 64

Racial superiority, German attitude of, 9, 16, 17n, 22
Radom, Poland, xv; prisoners from, 92
Rajewski, Ludwik, 25n, 84n, 86n, 112n
Rajsko subcamp, 70
Rationalizations to reduce guilt, 49
Red Cross activities, 115
Red triangular badges: meaning of, 85, 86-87, 106; of Polish political prisoners, 90; predominant in camp, 88
Reduction of needs, 127-128, 138, 141
Religious faith, as basis for resistance, 88-89, 133, 136
Rescue: hope for, 52; moral significance of, 12-13; via the resistance movement, 113, 121; strategy for, 107
Resistance: Auschwitz motto of, 127, 129; based on humanist values, 6-7, 11-14, 133-134, 136-137; relative to food, 76, 128; by Germans, 122; inner resources of man for, 2, 128-134; by Jehovah's Witnesses, 88-89; by maintaining sense of inner freedom, 127, 128, 132-133; patriotism and moral convictions as basis for, xv-xvi, 136-137; sense of humor for 129, 130, 132; values as frame of reference for, xxix, 133-134, 136-137. See also Self-defense mechanisms
Resistance movement, 112-122: communication systems in, 116, 119; defense mechanisms to sustain mental endurance promoted by, 119-120; contacts with the outside world, 109, 113, 114, 115; documents and information transmitted to the outside world by, 115, 116; gradual seizure of power by, 107; ideological and political goals of, 113, 114; as an international organization, 115; knowledge of SS officials used by, 109-110; national barriers overcome by, 117; organized compared to

spontaneous forms of, 114-115, 117, 118; origins of within Auschwitz, 108-109; reasons for strength of in Poland, 11-14, 136; role of Poles in, 12, 90, 113-114, 136-137; structure of, 113, 117-120; use of camp work site for, 40; use of triangular badges to hinder, 86; value judgments applied to participation in, 120-122
Revier. See Hospital
Risk-taking: capacity for, 63-64; determinants of, 130; results of, 64; stimulated by prisoners with loved ones, 96, 98; by underground organizations, 112-113
Roll call: death during, 76; described, 147; long duration of, 28, 68, 70, 147; penal, 129-130, 147
"Roosts:" adherence to rules for, 128; cooperation among prisoners sleeping on the same, 117; description of, 28, 29, 41; familial groups in, 33-34, 40
Round-ups, xviii, 58, 86, 87; described, 147
Russia: role of in Polish struggles for independence, xii, xiii-xiv, xv; seizure of Lithuanian and Ukrainian territories by, xiii-xiv
Russian prisoners, 16; loyalty and unity of groups of, 90; mass murder of, 54, 54n-55n; registered at Auschwitz, 25
Ryszka, Franciszek, 7n

Sabato, Ernest, quoted on irrational hope, xxix-xxx, 100
Sabotage, 116-117
Sachsenhausen, Germany, 106
Sadism, 20, 47, 78
Sanitation. See Unsanitary conditions
Sawicki, Jerzy, 21n
Scheisskommando, 129
Schools, in occupied Poland, xiv, xvii. See also Education
Schreibstube, 107
Scientists, prisoners as, 70n
Secrecy: of the extermination camps, 115; of great love relationships in

camp, 97; of Nazi criminal activities, 17–18, 21–22, 23, 78, 83
Selection of prisoners for death, 147; breaking the ban against leaving the barracks for, 35; criteria for and methods of, 54n–55n, 73–74; defense mechanisms for, 129–130; witnesses of, 79, 93; by SS doctors, 78, 147
Self-defense mechanisms, 126–134; by accepting reduced material needs, 127–128, 138, 141; attitudes toward death as, 77, 79–80, 131–132; belief in humanist values, 133–134; character traits conducive to cooperation as, 63, 130–131; humor as, 61, 126, 129, 130, 132; imagination as, 132–133; importance of, 85; and initiation into camp life, 60–67 *passim*; inner freedom as, 127, 128, 132–133, 141; revisions in traditional value systems for, 138–144; role of personality in, 59, 63–65, 126. *See also* Adaptation to camp life
Self-destruction, 127. *See also* Suicide
Self-reliance, 122
Self-worth, 49, 97
Serial numbers: significance of "old numbers," 58, 92; and social identity, 60; tattooing of, 60, 87, 92
Sewage disposal crews, 70; and adaptation to camp life, 129
Sexual deviants: among SS functionaries, 19; survival chances of, 57; triangular badges worn by, 86
Sexual distinctions, 53, 98
Sexual drives: of prisoner-functionaries, 98, 99; and homosexuality, 98–99; of "bosses" of women's crews, 65; extinguished via starvation, 98, 142
Shestov, Lev, xxx
Shock. *See* Psychic shock
Shoes: acquisition of, 77, 101, 104; in camp market, 104; inadequacy of, 41, 128
Siberia, xvi
Sicherheitsverwahrung (SV-ers), 87, 148
Silesia, 25
Singers, 119

Slave labor: concentration-camp prisoners used for, 15–17, 22, 56; deportations for, xv, xviii; and dysfunctional social norms, 143; survival of prisoners used for, 56–57, 62–64, 117
Slavs: murder of, 54; Nazi plan to sterilize, 54, 55n; as subhuman, xviii
Sleeping places, 117, 128; acquired via power in small groups, 62; as an article of trade in the camp market, 102; conflicts among prisoners during distribution of, 66; as location for consolidating groups of prisoners, 33–34, 40, 42
Slovakia, 91
Small groups. *See* Groups of prisoners
Smoke over Birkenau (S. Szmaglewska), xxv
Soap: manufactured from ashes of burned bodies, 17n, 54n; ownership of, 128
Social barriers: diminished by the camp market, 103–105, 109–111; diminished by stable work crews, 70–72
Social differentiation among prisoners: conflicts among prisoners caused by, 65–66; immense range of, 135: role of in relations between prisoners and SS officials, 71; and survival chances, 51–59
Social engineering, Nazi, 124–127; reasons for failure of, 127, 136; results of, 124–125, 127; as underestimating the strength of the Polish Resistance Movement, 136
Social experiment, Nazi: concentration camp as, 123–127; judging morality of prisoners in, 143; purposes of, 137; reasons for failure of, 127, 136
Social malfunctions, in the prisoners' environment, 124, 125
Socialist values, 139, 141
Socio-economic defense mechanisms, 100–111
Sociological approach to concentration camps, xxi, 6
Soła River, 25

Solidarity among prisoners: and disorientation caused by erroneous meanings of badges, 86–87; in groups of inmates from the same prison, 58; methods to abolish, 44–50; in neighboring bunks or "roosts," 33–34, 40, 42, 117; promoted by individual and collective methods for self-defense, 127–134; reduced by class and national antagonisms, 65–66; in work crews, 37, 40–41, 69–72. *See also* Bonds among prisoners; Groups of prisoners

Solitude, 62, 63

Sonderkommando, 77n; defined, 147; information transmitted by, 79; preserved documents of, 78; revolt of, 115

Soviet Union. *See* Russia

Spacial divisions: and erotic fulfillment among loved ones, 98; allowing groups of prisoners to communicate and to form groups, 33–34, 37, 40, 42, 117; and homosexuality, 98; as perceived by camp prisoners, 41–42

"Special treatment" symbol: meaning of, 60, 148; prisoners in penal crew because of, 64

Spontaneous resistance: to provide aid, xxix, 101, 119, 129–130, 136; compared to organized resistance, 114–115, 117, 118; values and convictions as basis for, xxix, 101, 136

Spoon, ownership of, 128

SS: evolution and power of, 147–148; German prisoners as deputies of, 57

SS functionaries: competition and antagonisms among, 21, 22–23; motives for choosing concentration camp-positions, 18–19; punishable deeds of, 21–22; recruitment for concentration-camp work, 20

SS officials: character traits of utilized by prisoners, 71, 84–85; childish dependency on, xxviii; cooperation between prisoner-functionaries and, 48–50; communication with prisoners, 70–71, 106, 109–111; drunken, 110; educated prisoners hated by, 56; greed for money among, 105; information obtained from, 116;

and love affairs among prisoners, 97; manipulated and influenced by prisoners, 71–72, 105, 109–111; number of at Auschwitz, 84–85; relationships with prisoners in stable work crews, 70–72

Stable personnel in work crews, 69–72

Starvation: causing theft of food, 66, 75–76; death from, 74–77; mental disturbances caused by, 125; psychological effects of, 74–77, 98, 142; and prisoners capable of resistance, 120. See also *Muselmänner*

State, Nazi: institutions of crime in, 15–23; supreme moral and legal authority of, 18

Stealing. *See* Theft

Steinbeck, John, xxvii

Sterilization: prisoners as test subjects for, 17; methods to test, 54, 55n

Storm troopers, 7–8

Strafkompanie. See Penal crews

Strength to resist terror, 122; creating feelings of, 129–130; from loved ones, 96, 97, 123, 133; internalized values as source of, xxix, 137; inner dialogues to create, 120. *See also* Self-defense mechanisms; Humanist values

Strzelecki, Jan, 112

Strzembosz, Tomasz, 6, 12–14, 13n

Subcamps: compared to city-states, 30, 33–35, 42; information transmitted among, 118, 119; isolation of, 71; prisoners allowed to circulate within and outside of, 118

Suicide, 13, 126. *See also* Self-destruction

Suffering: effects of, 5; and evil, xxx; by prisoners with loved ones, 94–95; religious mystique of, xxiii; self-defense mechanism for, 132

Survival: attitudes toward death to promote, 77, 80, 131–132; defensive adaptations for, 126–134; evaluation of behavior for, xxvii–xxix, 138–144; via homosexuality, 99; indicated by "old numbers," 92; spontaneous behavior for, 100–101; via theft, 66, 75–76, 142; uncompromising pursuit of, 49, 50

Survival chances, 51-67; arrival time in camp as a determinant in, 58-59; economic differences among prisoners as factor in, 55; educational and occupational factors in, 55-57; enhanced by aid for newcomers from old prisoners, 61-62; enhanced by working in stable work crews, 69-72; increased by obtaining specialized camp functions, 106, 108-109; increased by the camp market, 101-105, 109-111; inequality of, 61-67; living conditions as method to reduce, 16; luck in, 67; nationality of prisoner as factor in, 54-55; of peasants, 56-57; of the physically weak, 53, 54n; role of psychological responses in, 59-64, 126-134; and social differentiation, 51-59; among work crews, 37, 40, 69-72, 129. *See also* Adaptation to camp life; Self-defense mechanisms

Survivor, The (Terrence Des Pres), xxvii

Survivors: children of, xxvii; human nature viewed by, 4; and the resistance movement, 121

"Sv-ers," 87, 148

Sympathy, expressions of, 65, 77, 101, 120

Szucha prison, 13

Tattooed numbers on prisoners, 60, 87, 92

Technology: for killing, 54n-55n, 78; social, 124-127

Ten Commandments, reinterpretation of, 141-142

Terror: ability to inflict, 5; to abolish cohesiveness of prisoner groups, 44-50; authority of, 7-10; and barriers between "persons" and "non-persons," 20-21, 72, 111; and changes in camp power structure, 108; collaboration with, 48-50, 128; defense mechanisms of prisoners to resist, 11-14, 61-67, 126-134; as liberating strength to resist, 122; in occupied Poland, xv-xviii, 11-14; organizational structure of based on industrialized mass murder, 77-80; in

the performance of work, 47; promoted by administrative divisions in camps, 33; psychic preparation for, 58; and the resistance movement, 113-122; social engineering for, 17, 124-125; of the stronger over the weaker, 66, 88

Teutsch, A., 61n

Theft: by prisoners, 65, 66, 75-76, 88, 104, 142; by prisoner-functionaries, 46; revised moral standards for, 142; by SS officials, 19, 21-22

Third Reich: criminal activities sanctioned by, 136; institutions of state crime under, 15-23; moral and legal authority of, 18-19; victims' possessions as property of, 21-22, 78, 103

Toilets: access to, 88; description of, 30; in prisoners' communication system, 34

Torture: fear of, 50; of political prisoners, 13; psychological collapse from, 126-127

Training, Nazi: of German youth, 9, 124, 137; moral degeneracy caused by, 9, 20; social technology used for, 124; of non-German children, xvii

Transports: groups of prisoners formed from, 62, 114, 119; seasonal arrivals of, 58-59; tattooed numbers indicate prisoners from the same, 92

Treason, 87

Triangular badges. *See* Colored triangular badges

Ukraine, xiii, xvi

Underground organizations, xiv, 87, 112-113, 120. *See also* Resistance movement

University of Warsaw, xix-xx, xxii

University professors, survival chances of, 56

Unsanitary conditions, adaptation to, 30, 46, 60, 128

Urban working class, survival chances of prisoners from, 56

Vagrants, as camp prisoners, 57, 85, 92

Value(s): acceptance of force as, 18-

19, 49, 124, 133–134; of aid for the weaker, 49, 53, 136; of assisting one's neighbor, 139, 141, 144; of a bond with the wronged, xxx, 144; conflict between civilized norms and values revised for camp conditions, 137–144; formed under conditions of extremity, 140; as a frame of reference for behavior of prisoner-functionaries, 48–50; as a frame of reference for resistance, 6–7, 11–14, 133–134, 136–137, 138–144; generated from concentration camps, xxx, 144; heroism achieved via, 121, 141, 144; internalized, xxv, xxix, 137; in Nazi Germany, 8–9; of old prisoners helping newcomers, 61–62; analyzed by A. Pawełczyńska, xxiv–xxv, xxix; reduced for survival, 137–144; for spontaneous resistance, xxix, 101, 136; prisoners' battles for, 3, 6, 11–14, 59, 101, 121–122, 133–134, 137, 140–141, 144; sustained by informal groups, 143–144; as a unifying bond among prisoners, 6–7, 11–14, 59, 121–122, 133–134, 136–137, 138–144. *See also* Humanist values

Value judgments: ability to form independent, 10, 20, 140; applied to participation in the resistance movement, 120–122; of survival behavior, xxiv–xxv, 137–138

Values and Violence (A. Pawełczyńska), xx; award earned by, xxiii; epigraphs at chapter heads in, xxvi, xxix–xxx; Polish edition of, xxi, xxv; Marxist and Catholic reviews of, xxiv–xxv; Polish reception of, xxiii–xxvi

Verbal abuse, 84, 138

Victims' possessions: in the camp market, 80, 102–103, 104–105; as property of the Third Reich, 21–22, 78, 103; sorted by prisoners, 78, 79, 93, 102–103, 107

Victory: from achieving inner freedom, 141; in the world of values, 121

Violence: expressions of protest against, 120, 137, 141; size of the apparatus for, 45, 84–85; of the stronger to the weaker, 66

Walk, relearning how to, 128

War Crimes Investigation Commission (Polish). *See* Główna Komisja Badania Zbrodni Hitlerowskich w Polsce

War criminals: society's moral judgment of, 3–4; trials of, 2–3. *See also* Criminal activities, Nazi

Warnings among prisoners: about SS officers, 84–85; transmitted by conspiratorial organizations, 116; about work as a method to promote death, 116–117

Warsaw, Poland: Nazi prisons in, 13–14, 92; University of, xxix–xx, xxii

Washrooms: access to, 30; role of in communication among prisoners, 34

Water, access to, 30, 46, 88, 128

Weak prisoners: attitudes of prisoner-functionaries toward, 49; extermination of, 53, 54n; protected by other prisoners, 63, 119

Weaker, the: terror of the stronger over, 66, 88; value of caring for, 49, 53, 136

Weakness, and maintaining norms, 140, 143

Weapons industry, 117

Wehrmacht officers, xvi

Weil, Simone, xxx–xxxi

Winkiel, defined, 148. *See also* Colored triangular badges

Winter transports, 58–59

Wolny, Jan, 112n

Women: barracks for, 28; camp for, 30, 45, 79, 90, 128; Greek Jewish, 126; male prisoners' protection of, 117; as prisoner-functionaries, 99, 109; sexual drives of "bosses" of, 65; shaven heads of, 60, 91; unity among Yugoslav female prisoners, 90–91; visit of the men's work crews to camp of, 99; washrooms for, 30

Work: adaptation to, 63, 129; conditions and locations for, 35–42, 69–72, 129; avoiding exhaustion from, 63, 116–117; not done by the camp elite, 81; performed under threat of terror, 63, 68; physical weakness preventing, 53, 54n; protection of weak prisoners during, 63, 119; road to, 37, 40, 41; and specialized camp functions, 70, 106–107, 108, 118; tempo of, 63, 116–117. *See also* Slave labor; Work crews

Work crews: authority of prisoner-functionaries over, 40, 41, 45, 47–48; communication among, 40, 42–43; cooperation among for mutual self-defense, 62–64, 71–72; composed of national groups, 64; composed primarily of men, 99; for hauling sewage, 129; passage through the camp gate by, 40–41; penal, 64, 69, 148; protection of weak prisoners in, 63, 119; small groups among, 40, 62–63; to sort plundered property, 102–103; influence over SS officials acquired by, 70–72; stable personnel in augments survival chances of, 69–72; supervisors of women's crews, 65; survival chances among, 37, 40, 62–64, 69–72. *See also* Field crews; *Sonderkommando*

Work site: inside the camp, 35, 37, 70; as place for communication, 37, 40, 42, 70–72; outside the camp, 37, 40–41, 42, 48; risk-taking activities at, 63–64

"Work will set you free," 116–117, 145

Wormser, Olga, 115n

Yellow triangular badges, 86, 91

Yugoslav prisoners, 90–91

Zauna. *See* Bathhouse

Zugänge, defined, 148. *See also* Newcomers

Zugangsbaracke, 62; defined, 148

Design	Al Burkhardt
Composition	Freedmen's Organization
Lithography	Halliday Lithograph Corp.
Binder	Halliday Lithograph Corp.
Text	Compugraphic English 49
Display	Jetsetter Helvetica Medium